Edited by

Arlington Heights Authors

A Collection of Stories and Poems
from a Midwest Writing Group

—

Volume 1

AHA !

A Collection of Stories and Poems
from a Midwest Writing Group

–

Volume 1

Contact us at: WritersPage.AlmanacLocal.com/aha.html

Several stories by Andrew Brand, Jim Elgas, and Larry King were previously published in *The Almanac of Arlington Heights,* 2001-2011. Several stores by William D. Hicks were also previously published, including: "Energy Services," in *Evernight,* July, 1997, "Why I Hate to Move," in *Mosaic,* June, 2011, "Siblings," in *The Wright Side,* September, 1997, and "Granny Goes to the Nursing Home," in *Mosaic,* 2006.

Cover design by Alisa Kober

Text design and composition by Curt Clapper

ISBN-10: 146792508X

ISBN-13: 978-1467925082

AHA!

BILL HICKS
JIM ELGAS
ALISA KOBER
CURT CLAPPER
ANDY BRAND
LARRY
KING

DEDICATION
with THANKS

*We are a few amiable folks who like to make things
and believe in the power of words and images.
We connected through the
Arlington Heights Memorial Library.*

*You gave us a clean, well-lighted space,
one surrounded by inspiration and encouragement.
The great good place.*

*Every great Library is a catalytic point
transforming individuals and communities.*

*The Arlington Heights Memorial Library
is a great Library, indeed.*

 CB

CONTENTS

Introduction

If you want to be a writer, write.
If you want to be a good writer, rewrite.

-Arlington Heights Authors, 2011

A common love for reading, writing, and libraries brought us together. The six of us, Alisa, Andy, Bill, Curt, Jim, and Larry, were already members of *The Writing Place*, a creative writers' group at our local Arlington Heights Memorial Library. Like the clichéd dream of so many aspiring authors, we shared the desire to be published. So we formed a second group, *Arlington Heights Authors*, with the goal of publishing some of our writing in book form.

However, if we wanted our works to be worthy of publication, we needed to make sure we were the authors of *good* writing. This meant writing, sharing, listening, and rewriting, a process that for most of these poems and stories transpired many times. For the two years we met, each of us brought different tastes, styles, and points of view, both to our own stories and to our critiques of the others'. Most stories in this book, then, came from each individual author but were molded into their final form after suggestions from the group.

Ultimately, our stew of ideas came together and ***AHA!*** was born.

ANDREW BRAND

Andy's Acknowledgements:

For as long as I can remember, stories have buzzed around my mind like flies trapped in an overturned jar. When I was younger, a few escaped by finding their way to paper, but sadly, most wasted away, suffocating somewhere in my memory. Then two years ago, I began writing short fiction for the quarterly *Almanac of Arlington Heights*. Most of the stories in *AHA!* were originally published there.

The first drafts of many of these stories were anything but short fiction. In many cases I had to cut characters, change locations, and sometimes completely rewrite story-lines. My goal for these later drafts was determining what the story was really about, and then making sure that was the story I told. Afterwards, I would bring what I thought was a final manuscript to our group only to have it changed further, always for the better.

Most of these stories were inspired by experiences from my life. Whether or not that original inspiration survived the final cut (and plenty did not), bits of my life are still strewn throughout. My hope is that these nuggets of truth help to make the stories more realistic, and paint a believable picture in the reader's mind.

There are many people who made this book possible. None the least of which are my fellow *AHA!* authors. Thanks for the critiques and the hard work. Thank you, also to the members of *The Writing Place*, as you have all helped me to tell better stories.

To Debbie, my wife, thank you for being such an ardent supporter of my writing. Also, a giant thanks for the countless times you've helped me find the word that was not quite on the tip of my tongue. You are the best! I love you. Finally, thank you, Colin, for your smiles, laughs and inspiration. I didn't realize until after you were born that you have always been part of my stories.

ANDREW BRAND

Margaritte's Snow

by Andrew Brand

The snow fell like flurries of floating fish. Schools of tiny flakes rode the winter breeze in a finely choreographed dance. Each swirled in the same direction at the same time.

Hank Watkins thought of his wife and sighed. Tonight would have been Marge's 73rd birthday. But this uniform snowfall was nothing like Marge. He'd been waiting for a sign. Maybe this was it.

Six years before, she lay in a hospital bed. Her mostly gray hair, with patches of dark brown, spread haphazardly across the pillow. She whispered in a voice only Hank could hear, "I'll always love you, Hank Watkins... sure as... I'm dying... I'll visit... promise... look for me... a sign..."

He had long wondered what that sign might be. Tonight he finally heard the answer in the resounding snowy silence. He realized the reason Marge hadn't sent a sign was because, except in memories, she no longer existed.

Back when they first met, he was awkward, 17 years old and went by "Henry." She was that beautiful brunette, almost 16. Called herself "Margaritte." Though she actually spelled it M-a-r-g-a-r-e-t, she said her name with a faux French accent.

They took the same ballroom dance class. Margaritte was

getting ready for her sweet-sixteen birthday party. Her younger brother was her dance partner. Likewise, Henry was his younger sister's escort for her own sweet-sixteen.

For seven weeks, the brothers and sisters suffered each other's company and that of their uptight instructor, Mr. Priggly. On week eight, Henry's sister was ill, as was Margaritte's brother. For that class, Margaritte and Henry were partners.

Standing so close, he could smell the flowery soap on her skin mixed with the outside coldness that came in with her. She leaned into him and whispered, "Follow my lead." The soft warmth of her breath on his ear forced Henry to do just that.

Margaritte danced nothing like his sister. She added swirls and flourishes discouraged by the stick-like Mr. Priggly. While the other teenagers were stiff wooden soldiers marching to set choreographies, Margaritte was a butterfly leading Henry across the wood floor with unpredictable and exhilarating movements. In the wall-length mirror, Henry simultaneously glimpsed his terrified smile, Margaritte's peaceful grin, and Mr. Priggly's disapproving frown.

When class ended, the two stood outside the dance studio in the blowing January snow. Margaritte waited for her father to pick her up. Henry waited beside her before walking home himself.

The wind whipped her hair while the sticking snow turned it from brown to white. He offered her his scarf and hat, but she declined. So Henry kept them in the pocket of his green parka, which he left unzipped with the hood down in an attempt to impress her.

"Look at the snowfall," she said. "It's perfect."

"Yeah," he said with a shiver, although he didn't notice anything perfect about it.

"All of these snowflakes," she continued. "All of them are doing something different. Falling and blowing every

4

which way. I absolutely love it."

Then her father plowed up to the curb in his blue Studebaker. She got into the car and waved. "See you later, Hank." That was the first time anyone had called him Hank. But, like the snow, it stuck.

"See you, *Margaret*." He smiled and waved.

As they drove off, she rolled down the window and shouted, "Margaritte!" and smiled back.

Even with the snow whipping and stinging his face, Henry did not wear his scarf or hat on the walk home. Instead he shielded himself with her name, repeating it like a song, "Margaritte, Margaritte, Margaritte." Those three syllables rolling off his tongue warmed him. He realized how perfect the blustery snow really was.

As the years passed, Margaritte became Maggie, then Meg, then Margaret and finally Marge. Constantly changing just like her dancing and her snowflakes.

Nearly 57 years later, from his living room window, Hank watched the perfectly uniform snow falling peacefully outside. A blue van with black and white lettering across the side shattered the calm, speeding recklessly down the snow-covered street. The snow in its wake flew every which way. The tiny flakes no longer followed each other in lock-step. They whirled and twirled in a chaotic upheaval.

That's the type of snow Marge would've loved, Hank thought.

It wasn't until he was in bed that he realized the name on the van that redirected the snowfall was *Margaritte's Catering*.

And that night, she paid Hank a visit in his dreams.

Paternal Force

by Andrew Brand

"Act tough. Confident," my dad said. He glanced to the action figures by the window. "Think less Luke Skywalker. More Han Solo." He nodded to the poster on the wall over my bed. "Maybe a dash of Darth Vader." He smiled, "Use the Force, Dale," and tousled my hair.

When he was gone I still had no idea how to ask Chrissy Higgins to the "Springtime in '79" junior high dance. Lounging atop my *Star Wars* bedspread, I contemplated his advice. I stared at the Darth Vader poster and the Han and Luke action figures on the windowsill. I wondered if Dad had ever asked a girl out when he was thirteen.

Ten minutes later, Mom flitted into my room with her knowing grin, a beacon of maternal energy. She sat on the edge of my bed, cupped her hands round my cheeks, and burst out with: "Oh, my little Daaaley! You have a giiirl-friend!"

I shook my head dislodging her hands. "She's not my girlfriend. I haven't even asked her to the dance yet."

"Daaaley, just be yourself. You'll be fine."

Dad appeared at the door. "Be like Han Solo. That's how I caught my little Princess Leia." He hitched his thumb toward Mom.

"Han Solo, huh?" She smirked and plucked the Luke

Skywalker figure off the windowsill. Mom sat dreamily for a moment, "You're growing up, Daley," then placed Luke down. He toppled over behind the bed. She hurried from my room and gestured to the orange phone on the hall table. "Want to call her now?"

Moments later, the orange phone cord was stretched taut into my bedroom. I sat against the door to keep it closed and my parents out. I stared at the Darth Vader poster and thought, Be. Han. Solo. A pit in my stomach grew with each ring of Chrissy Higgins's phone.

"Hello?" Chrissy answered.

"Chrissy." I sounded more surprised than confident. I heard her soft rhythmic breathing. "Chrissy," I repeated louder. I just said Chrissy Higgins's name twice and breathing was her only response. I panicked and said it again even louder, "Chrissy!" Unsure how to fix the damage I'd already done, I dove right in: "Doyouwannago-tothespringdancewithme?"

"Excuse me?" It sounded like she coughed, which I hoped was more promising than her breathing.

I tried it slower. "Doyou-wanna-goto-thespringdance-withme?"

"Do I want to go to...what?" She was obviously trying to torture me.

"The spring dance— with me." I was not Han Solo. Not confident or tough. Darth Vader glowered down at me.

"Who is this?" Chrissy asked.

I am an idiot. I never even said my name.

Before I could say anything, there was a click. Dad's voice came from another extension. "Dale, are you on the phone?"

"Dale? From science class?"

"Dad!"

"Dale, I'm already going to the dance with Jack Sloan," Chrissy said and hung up. The phone went silent, except for Dad's Vader-like breathing.

"Thanks a lot, Dad. Way to help me out." I shoved the phone through the cracked open door and let it fall to the ground. I pushed hard on the door. It shut with an unsatisfying thud. The nervous pit in my stomach had become an angry void.

I lunged at the Darth Vader poster and ripped it down. It tore at the corner leaving the left side of Vader's helmet on the wall. I seized Han Solo, twisted off his head and whipped the action figure across the room. I yanked the *Star Wars* comforter off my bed and flung it at the door.

Dad was standing there. The bedspread hit him in the chest. "Sorry about the phone, Dale. I— "

"I don't want hear it," I yelled. Angry tears escaped from my eyes, making me angrier still. "You made me look like an idiot!"

Dad picked up the headless Han Solo. "Maybe my advice wasn't so great. Thinking about *Star Wars* when asking out a girl isn't... Well, girls just don't get *Star Wars*."

I collapsed onto my disheveled bed— beaten. "Even still." I wiped my tears. "I wasn't tough or confident."

"No, Dale, you don't need to be tough and confident to ask a girl out." Dad offered a weak smile. "You need it after she shoots you down."

Early Gifts

by Andrew Brand

My seven-year-old daughter, Melanie, stares up at me with her blue moon caught-in-the-act eyes. Tears spill over her eyelashes and down her cheeks while a panicked anxiety washes over me. She just found the stash of Christmas presents under her mother's and my bed, and I realize this is a moment she will remember for the rest of her life. What's a father supposed to do in this situation? I contemplate calling downstairs to my wife and passing the whole thing off to her, when I notice how much Melanie, with those beautiful blue eyes and long red hair, reminds me of her Aunt Georgia.

Georgia is my younger sister. We haven't spoken in years, not since our parents passed away. Sorrow, fatigue, my pride, and, of course, money did in our sibling relationship. At the time, Melanie was only a few months old. She never got to know the aunt she so resembles.

When Georgia was six years old she begged me to go with her and see Santa Claus. My mother, who must have sensed the Santa-doubt creeping through my eight-year-old body, stared me down and willed me to say, "Sure, I'll go with you, Georgia. How else would Santa know what I want?"

As I sat on Santa's lap at Wiebolt's Department Store, my doubts were only intensified by the old guy's fake beard, the smell of mouthwash and cigarettes on his breath, and the unbridled wafts of Old Spice. Whether or not Santa really existed, I knew this Wiebolt's Santa was a farce. Georgia, on the other hand, just smiled with giddy excitement when she sat on his lap, putting all her faith into this stranger masquerading in a red suit.

Three days before Christmas, Georgia and I played hide and seek in the house. I found her sitting in my parents' closet amidst a pile of wrapped presents. She opened the label on one package wrapped in red and green paper, *To: Georgia - From: Santa*, written in my mom's script. Then next to it, another bigger box in snowman paper, *To: Josh - From: Santa*, written by my dad. A dozen more gifts sat on top of them and, in my mind, added up to only one possibility.

Georgia turned to me with wide-eyed excitement and laughed. "Santa came early."

"Santa?" I said, "That's Mom and Dad's handwriting on the labels." I didn't mean to blurt it out like that, although honestly, I felt the evidence should have been pretty compelling even to my six-year-old sister.

Georgia shook her head and spoke very slowly, as if I were a dimwitted younger brother. "Joshua, it's not like Santa really flies around the world in one night. Even I know that's not possible. He probably delivered these earlier and asked Mommy and Daddy to hide them until Christmas."

For a brief moment, I had an arrogant urge to crush her little dream. Then she smiled at me. I looked into her gorgeous blue eyes framed by her flowing red hair, and decided to give Georgia an early Christmas gift— the gift of innocence, at least for one more year. "That makes sense, Georgia. You must be right."

So now, one week before Christmas, my daughter, having found her presents, looks up at me with her own blue eyes and a tear stained face. She sobs, clutching her arms around my neck. "Santa really doesn't exist. Just like Timmy at school said."

I pause and silently curse this little Timmy, then I thank Georgia because I realize I wasn't the only one giving an early Christmas gift so long ago. Although she couldn't have realized it and certainly didn't plan it, Georgia gave me an early present too. I simply had to wait twenty-nine years in order to use it.

I kiss Melanie's head and turn her chin up toward my face. "Honey, Santa dropped these gifts off early." I smile. "He was very busy so he asked Mommy and me to hide them until Christmas."

Melanie stares at me a long ten seconds, weighing my sincerity. After a final snuffled breath, she smiles, and runs off into her seven-year-old world.

Afterwards, I call my sister but not without some trepidation. "Merry Christmas, Georgia," I say, startled at the tears welling up in my eyes. "I miss you, Sis."

Her breath catches. "Joshua," she says. Then I hear a smile form in her voice. "It's been too long."

Half Empty

by Andrew Brand

Her long blonde hair, pulled back into a bow the way pretty young women always seemed to know how to do, tortured Charlie Hamilton. It wasn't just her hair. It was that the pretty young co-ed in the bright pink Hawaiian shirt stood in line with so many other college students getting ready to board a Spring Break flight to South Padre. And that the flight was leaving from Chicago. Charlie had no feelings of desire toward this young woman, although she was very attractive. Instead, as with all pretty blondes he noticed, Charlie felt a longing for lost years. Like a child getting walloped by brain freeze after eating ice cream too quickly, Charlie reveled in the taste of his memories but loathed the languishing pain that accompanied them.

He was killing some time in O'Brien's Pub across from gate H5 at O'Hare before his 12:30 flight to Minneapolis. His torturous week without a sale mercifully ended early, so now Charlie lounged with his loosened tie lolling over his belly while his gray suit coat hung from the back of his barstool. Before he noticed the pretty college girl, he had been mentally preparing for yet another lonely weekend watching recorded television shows.

"South Padre, here we come!" one boisterous college boy shouted from across the hall. A cheer of celebration erupted from the other students.

The bartender, wearing a white shirt, black vest, and bowtie, was an older woman with a worn face and dark graying hair. She frowned when the college boy shouted his departure cry, then glanced across the mahogany bar to Charlie's $12 vodka tonic. She said nothing, as his tumbler was still half full. Since the clock behind the bar read two hours shy of noon, Charlie supposed his drink, like the rest of his life, was more aptly referred to as half empty.

Charlie had trouble believing he'd ever been as carefree and callow as those college students, but the co-ed in the pink Hawaiian shirt reminded him that he had. She reminded him of Monica-from-Chicago, whose last name he never knew, just a Spring Break fling that, in retrospect, was the best week of his life.

As a senior at the University of Minnesota, Charlie met Monica-from-Chicago on the beaches of South Padre Island during the only Spring Break excursion he'd ever taken. They got on swimmingly. Her dazzling sapphire eyes sparkled bluer than the warm Gulf waters in which she first flirted with him. Twenty-two years later, the memory of lathering suntan lotion over her perfectly proportioned body still made Charlie swoon. They spent four fun-filled days and passionate nights together. She was a princess; he was a toad. Since then, no other woman had come close to transforming Charlie into a prince the way Monica had.

Two years after graduation, he was in Chicago on business and briefly thought he saw Monica stepping onto a bus at a crowded corner. When Charlie realized it wasn't her, his disappointment both surprised and overwhelmed him. The woman was heavier than Monica and not so put together, but there was enough of a resemblance to make Charlie do a double take as he drove by.

"There's quite a resemblance," the bartender's husky voice snapped Charlie from the memory, as if reading his mind. She smiled, "At first I thought you were a creep. Staring at her that way. Then I caught a glimpse of her face. It made perfect sense."

Charlie gave her a confused look.

"That girl over there. The one headed to Spring Break." She nodded toward the pretty co-ed. "I mean— she is the spitting image of you. Prettier though. You're keeping tabs on her, making sure she gets off okay. You're her dad. Right?"

Charlie struggled with the bartender's words, trying to make sense of them. He looked back to the young woman. She appeared to be about twenty-one years old.

"She is your daughter. Isn't she?" the bartender asked.

Without warning, Charlie leapt up and ran across the hall. He had no plan in mind, only questions: *Is Monica your mother? Who's your father? Me?* Yet all he could shout was, "Hey!" A few people in line turned toward him and frowned, but the pretty young co-ed had already stepped through the door leading to the jetway.

Crestfallen, Charlie returned to the bar.

The bartender smiled wanly. "You want another?" She pointed to his now completely empty vodka tonic.

"Make it a double," Charlie said.

The Third Miracle

By Andrew Brand

"Look, Daddy. Your reindeer."

My parents, the outdoorsy agnostics that they were, loved to go camping on Christmas. Junior year in high school, they took me to Point Reyes National Park in northern California, a coastland wilderness where salt, ocean, and pine perfumed the mild winter air. At night, the indigo sky shimmered with a quilt of countless sparkling stars that disappeared behind the spires of pine-covered bluffs.

Late Christmas Eve, after a long day of hiking, I woke in my pup tent to a distant animal's cry, floating just under the whispered breaths of the coastal waves. I decided to investigate the low grunting moan while my parents, in their own tent, remained oblivious and continued a synchronized snoring routine.

I grabbed a lantern and headed into the forest toward the mournful cry. Twigs snapped. Trees creaked. The dark forest frightened me more than I wanted to admit. I kept my free hand on the hunting knife hanging from my belt. I almost turned back twice, but both times the animal's wailing pulled me forward. After scraping past hundreds of bushes and trees, I came to a clearing where the animal's din became so loud that it drowned out the rhythmic song of the ocean and the percussive creaks of the forest.

I stepped forward tentatively into the small meadow. There, a large elk lay on the ground like the fossil of some fallen dinosaur. Its grey and brown pelt rose and fell with each tortured cry. Huffing and snorting and howling. The animal seemed tired and in pain although I couldn't see why. Carefully, I walked to it, knelt down, and stroked its head. It's okay, I told it.

The elk continued wailing then kicked its back legs as if looking for a comfortable position. I lifted the lantern and saw a pair of smaller rear legs sticking out from between the larger ones. This elk was giving birth. Just like the time on my grandparents' farm when a calf was born rear legs first. Realizing that the baby cow was stuck, my grandfather pulled it out by its legs. Recalling what Grandpa did, I cautiously walked to the rear of the elk, grabbed the two smaller hoofed legs and pulled. At first, my hands slipped off. The legs were covered in a wet birthing slime. I grimaced and wiped my hands on my brown sweatshirt. Then I pulled off the sweatshirt, wrapped it around the baby elk's legs, and yanked harder. The tiny elk popped loose and slid out of its mama. The mother stopped howling and lifted her head as if to see what had just happened. Then, she shifted toward the calf and began licking it.

As the baby lay on my sweatshirt, I realized its pelt was completely white. An albino. The mother took no heed and lovingly nuzzled it. When the calf began to nurse, an unexpected rush of emotions overwhelmed me. My eyes welled up. I stayed with the elk until the morning birds sang. Then, leaving my soiled sweatshirt, I trekked back to camp in an awestruck stupor.

I told my parents the whole thing. They didn't believe me. Elk don't give birth in winter, my dad said. When I couldn't find that meadow again, they thought I made it up as an excuse for losing my sweatshirt. But I knew what happened. What I did. To me it was a miracle and on Christmas no less.

Seven years later, my son was born. I cried then too.

And seven years after that, I took him to Point Reyes. He knew my story. I told him elk were like reindeer. So when a young elk walked out from the foliage, he pointed and said, "Look, Daddy. Your reindeer."

This little elk had brown fur with patches of white across its back and tiny nubs for antlers. I knew the calf could not be the same baby elk from fourteen years ago. Yet I wished it were, so I could truly share that magical moment with my son. Then a second animal walked out from the underbrush. A large elk with full-grown antlers—albino white. It corralled the calf protectively. Then in a surreal moment, the white elk knowingly tilted its head toward me. We both stared: two fathers with our sons. After a minute, they walked back into the forest.

And the tears fell from my eyes as I hugged my son tight.

Mocha and Mirrors

by Andrew Brand

Whenever busybody customers asked Lenora why her nose, lips, and eyebrows were pierced she replied, "Because I like pain. Which is why I'm the barista here at Cathy's Coffee Café." And while making their coffee she would repeat to herself, "The customer's always trite."

Lenora's nametag, made by her dolt of a boss, read *Nora*. Despite her protests, customers insisted on using the amputated name.

"My espresso's too hot, Nora."

"This latte's too cold, Nora."

"Nora, this cocoa's not right."

She'd never had her fingernails pulled out, but Lenora was certain waiting on customers was just as agonizing. Her favorite time of the workday was between 9:30 and 11:30 AM— the dead hours, she called them. That was when the shop was usually empty.

An older man with a vapid expression showed up at the counter of the otherwise empty café at 10:15 on one dreary Monday. Lenora had not seen or heard him enter and her reaction of, "Where'd you come from?" was as much from surprise as annoyance.

The man looked to be in his late sixties. He wore a plain white baseball cap, high-waisted dark jeans, and a blue denim jacket.

"Where am I?" he said in a dazed voice with a Slavic accent.

Lenora realized that whatever this guy needed was not behind the counter. "I just serve coffee, guy."

"I was staring at my reflection in the water and I... I must have fallen in." He looked down at his perfectly dry clothes.

"What do you want?" Lenora said.

He glanced at her nametag. "Nora."

"The name's Lenora. I hate 'Nora'." With her middle finger she mimicked crossing out *Nora* on the nametag. "So what do you want?"

He stared at her.

"Do you want coffee?" she sighed.

"There are no mirrors," the man said looking around. "How did I get here?"

"Okay, you are officially creeping me out. Order or leave."

He whispered, "The lagoon."

"I need a mocha," she said and went to make the drink, hoping he might leave if she ignored him.

As she turned he asked, "Do you like mirrors, Nora?"

Trying to ignore him, she stifled her invective.

"Mirrors show the truth. No way to hide from unhappiness when it stares at you in the mirror. I know. For thirty years I made mirrors in my shop."

By the time she finished making the mocha, he had stopped talking and was standing by a table at the front of the café, staring down at an opened *Sun-Times*.

"Okay, time to leave," Lenora said with a nod toward the door.

"Drag the Lincoln Park Lagoon," he said and tapped the newspaper.

"Say what?" she asked.

He turned toward the front window then walked right

into it without so much as a thud. He was gone.

Lenora gaped. She might have blinked, but she didn't think so. The crazy Slavic mirror guy disappeared right before her eyes.

"Like Doug-frickin-Henning," she said and slurped the mocha.

She walked to the front table. It was empty except for the newspaper. She glanced down and noticed the title of an article on the open page:

MIRROR MAN MISSING

**Denis Slovatnitz, owner of Glass and Mirror
Designs, disappeared two weeks ago...**

A flicker of movement made Lenora look up, but the sidewalk outside the café was empty. She had merely glimpsed her translucent reflection in the front window. Then just beyond her reflection but still in the window, she noticed a ghostly image of Denis Slovatnitz walking away.

She flipped the paper to the classifieds. "I need a new job."

A Memory

by Andrew Brand

I shouldn't be afraid of the dark. I'm a forty-nine year old plumber for crissake. I've worked plenty of times in places darker than this. My wife, she ain't scared. She's asleep right next to me and won't wake up for nothing. If it weren't for her damned question back at dinner, maybe I'd be asleep right now, too.

"What's your earliest memory?" she asked me.

I thought about it, swallowed some casserole, then said, "Christmas. Four years old. I got a G.I. Joe that year." Except I knew there was an earlier memory. One I couldn't find at dinner, but I could sense it way in the back of my mind, trying to move forward.

Now, in the darkness of our bedroom, it found me and I can't sleep.

I was in my crib for an afternoon nap. Couldn't have been more than three years old. My brother and two sisters were downstairs counting Halloween candy from the day before. My parents kept shushing them. Saying not to wake me up.

But I wasn't asleep. Through the closed bedroom door, I could hear all their chattering.

Then the door creaked open.

Through the slats of my crib, I noticed a crack of light

from the hallway. A soft glow that brightened the edge of the pale blue door, revealing its color. With the shades drawn, the rest of my room was gray and dark. Yellow dresser, blue hamper, purple blanket, all of them looked like the black and white picture from our television set. Except near that sliver of light. That's where I first noticed her fingers.

They crept around the edge of the door, all spindly and green like bony rigid snakes searching for a meal. Her finger-nails, long and dingy yellow, looked like they'd never been manicured.

Next, her face came peeking around the edge of the door. Crazed blood-shot eyes with bushy, pointed eyebrows, a crooked nose with a wart on it, just like a kid's mask. But this wasn't no mask, and she wasn't looking for candy. I knew that much.

She looked straight at me in my crib, showing her rotten yellow teeth through a twisted grimacing smile. She cackled in a whisper and seemed to glide toward me the rest of the way into the room. Her scraggly gray hair and pointed black hat traced a jagged frame around her shriveled lime-colored face.

From the long hanging sleeves of her black robe, two mossy gnarled hands writhed in rigid anticipation as they reached into my crib. Up close, the fingernails looked even more grotesque. Layered with tiny blistering bumps, bits of coarse black hair poked out from under the crustacean-like coverings.

As her hands came near me in the crib, I tried screaming but couldn't. The pointed fingernail of her index finger poked me. A stinging, yet tingling tickle ran through my whole body, and I began to laugh. Not a laugh with sound. No, it was the type of laugh where you can't make a noise, let alone breathe. Throughout the torture from her tickling-prickling appendages, my lungs burned. No matter how hard I tried, I couldn't break through the paralyzing laughter to suck in any air.

She brought her face to mine. The stench of rotten teeth and fetid meat slapped me. But I was in such anguish from my muted suffocation that I couldn't recoil from the horrible odor.

She hissed into my ear, "You don't remember me, but you will. Now that I've finally found you, it's my turn."

I didn't know what she meant, but I know that's what she said. I remember it clearly. Next thing I remember was my mom throwing open the door. The witch disappeared instantly. I was crying and my mom was trying to console me, saying something about a nightmare.

But it wasn't no nightmare. It happened.

I'd buried that memory away. Now it's back, and I'm scared to close my eyes. I watch my wife breathing deeply while she slumbers next to me. She won't wake up no matter how much I shake her.

The door to our bedroom just creaked open.

Packing Snow

by Andrew Brand

Five year old Karl stood atop a rickety seven foot ladder staring down into the giant red dumpster filled to the brim with white packing peanuts. Since the bits of Styrofoam were round, not peanut shaped, his dad, who worked in the Styrofoam factory, called them packing snow.

Karl had hoped to play in the pit of colorful plastic balls at the local McDonald's, but mom denied him, saying, "You'll just get sick from all the little monsters that have been in there." So instead, dad snuck him into the warehouse on a cold Sunday morning. "There are no monsters in here," his dad's voice echoed through the empty factory, "unless my boss catches us." His gruff laugh turned into a phlegm-filled smoker's hack.

The dumpster filled with packing snow stood six feet high, ten feet wide, and fifteen feet long. Karl, not intimidated by the dumpster's size, jumped off the ladder. As he fell through the air, he thought the Styrofoam really did look like snow. He hit it straight on. Packing snow exploded around him then tumbled over him in an avalanche as he sank into the dumpster. Snow covered his head blotting out the factory's flickering florescent lights, as he gently slid to the bottom into pure darkness. Karl marveled at how all that white looked so black from below. Then he heard a breath echoing just behind his own. He remembered his mom's warnings about the monsters in the McDonald's pit. Maybe one was here too, a monster hiding in the darkness between the snow.

Its breath surrounded him. "Karl", the monster hissed in a muffled raspy voice, "I'm coming after you". Karl tried to swim up to the top of the dumpster, but the monster snagged his shoelace. Karl kicked, trying to free himself. It held tight. He screamed. Something grabbed his arm and wrenched him up. He felt the shoelace grow taut then snap like a fishing line caught on a rock. His father lifted him to safety, but Karl knew the monster was still there, hiding in that packing snow.

He never mentioned the monster to anyone, afraid that talking about it might summon the beast. He even prayed his dad would quit working at the Styrofoam factory because the monster might follow him home. Then in the middle of January, Dad was "late off" so he couldn't work at the warehouse anymore. Karl wanted to rejoice but feared the monster had already followed Dad home because every night its ragged voice haunted Karl's nightmares. When he awoke, he could still feel the monster reaching inside him, coiling around his lungs and stomach. His parents knew about the monster too. While they argued late one night, Karl heard them call it a Says-shun. The monster was why they were always so angry at each other now. Karl was sure they would stop fighting if they just moved and got away from the Says-shun monster.

One month later, his parents said the three of them had to move into his grandparents' house. Their house had been "four closed." Whatever that meant. Karl didn't care, he was just thankful to move out.

After a week of sleeping on the pullout bed in Nana and Papa's small living room, Karl woke up from a nightmare and heard the grown-ups talking at the kitchen table. Through the hazy light in the doorway he could make out the dark outline of his dad hunched over the table, rubbing his eyes and smoking a cigarette. Their voices were quiet but tense. Karl sprung from the sofa bed.

"Stop talking about it," he shouted. "It will find us again."

Everyone turned to look at Karl in the doorway. He noticed his dad's cigarette fall to the floor leaving a trail of acrid smoke.

"What will find us, Sweety?" his mom asked.

"The monster," Karl whispered. "If you say its name it'll find us again."

"What on earth are you talking about?" Nana asked.

Karl whispered even softer, "The Says-shun monster. It came from daddy's work and found us in our old house."

"The Session monster?" His dad said, picking up the cigarette and taking a drag.

"He must mean the Re-session monster," Papa said and started laughing.

"Sweety," his mom smiled, "the recession isn't a monster."

"It is too," his dad growled.

Hiding between the words of Daddy's raspy voice, Karl heard it. The Recession had found them again.

Murphy's Stream

by Andrew Brand

The letter only had twenty-one words, but it brought me back fifty years. Once again ten years old trying to understand that strange complicated friendship.

During those long lazy summers, Jason Smith and me spent most our time across town in Old Man Murphy's barren field. Jason delighted in crushing grasshoppers like Godzilla stomping army tanks in Tokyo. "They eat the crops," he always said— an excuse that might've made sense had milkweed and crabgrass been considered crops.

On that day, we sat on a crumbling cement slab, looking down at Murphy's Stream, which was really just a drainage ditch on the south end of the field. The giant slab was stuck into the spongy ground of the weed-covered ravine.

A resident mother duck and her six ducklings swam around in the steady flow of water coming from a three-foot wide drainage pipe. Across the ravine about ten feet beyond the ducks was an ancient rusted wheelbarrow. Me and Jason could spend hours chucking rocks at that old iron beast. Sometimes we even hit it.

"Timmy, betchya can't hit it with your glasses off," Jason said to me. He was right of course. Without my thick Coke bottles I could barely see him sitting next to me, let alone the wheelbarrow. But I knew the etiquette of "betchya can't" and immediately accepted his challenge.

"Just point me in the right direction," I said and picked up a fist-sized chunk of cement. I turned toward the wheelbarrow and handed my glasses to Jason. "Watch this."

I threw the cement hard as I could but an instant later heard only the disappointing kerplunk of my cement hitting the stream. Then a second fluttering kerplunk.

Jason howled, "Man, you hit a baby duck!"

I put my glasses back on and was horrified to see the momma duck and only five of her babies scattering. One poor duckling floated lifelessly, spinning in the weak current.

"I...I didn't mean to..." I said. "I'm sorry...I..."

"Aw, it's just a duck," Jason said.

"Yeah, but..."

"Don't worry. People hunt 'em all the time."

"But it's...it's a baby." Tears welled up in my eyes.

"Look, if you want to beat yourself up, try this." Jason reached into his back pocket and pulled out something small, red and rectangular. "I swiped this nine volt battery from my pa's transistor radio. If you give it a lick, it'll shock that guilt right outta you."

That wasn't the type of penance I was looking for.

Jason could tell. "I bet you. You lost. And you hit that poor defenseless baby duck. You have to lick the battery." His smug "you have to" suggested he'd laid out a logic that I could not refute.

And I couldn't. I grabbed the battery. It had lightning bolts and that evil-looking black cat on the front. As I brought it toward my mouth, the two round contacts reminded me of some alien space pod ready to shoot lasers at me. I paused for a moment.

"C'mon. Chicken." Jason said.

I stuck my tongue out at him then pushed the contacts against it.

A sharp pop reverberated through my tongue and teeth.

A zap not at all pleasant but not as horrible as I'd expected either. Still, my knees felt obliged to buckle.

I lost my balance and tumbled down into Murphy's Stream. My glasses flew off. Sitting in the water, I couldn't see him, but I heard Jason laughing hysterically, sounding like some warped skipping record. I could handle my numb tongue and that taste of copper. I could handle the soaking wet. But Jason's soulless laugh chilled my blood.

Something rubbed against my arm and I flinched. The dead duckling had drifted into me. Jason continued laughing, and from under the wheelbarrow the blurry momma duck scowled at me. Without warning, a horrific guilt exploded from my chest in heaving sobs. Jason's laughter slowly faded. He was walking away.

We never spoke again.

I didn't question how he got my address from prison. After all, the reporters found me during his trial. I told them the truth. "I haven't seen Jason in forty years." Then I lied. "But it's hard to believe he's a killer."

The news said he didn't have any last words, but I received his letter this morning.

Timmy, I threw a rock too. It was mine that killed the duckling. Now, it's my turn to lick the battery.

Thin Air

by Andrew Brand

Lawrence Walters disappeared on Sunday, August twenty-third, year of our Lord 1868. The adults worried and fussed, like maybe a Pied Piper had taken him. I'd never tell them, but the truth was stranger than that. Anyhow, a Pied Piper would have returned Lawrence Walters straightaway. That boy was a mean-spirited blowhard, always threatening, pushing, and punching.

I was twelve years old that summer. Two months before he disappeared, I sat air tracing the gnarled old oak tree on a hill up past our Wesleyan Methodist church. Lawrence Walters snuck up behind me and without warning sliced off the curly blonde pigtail on my left side. Then he ran off cackling my name like a crazed coyote, "Ha! Eleanor Richardson!" For weeks, I mourned that missing hair with spiteful tears.

I shouldn't have been so surprised. I always knew if Lawrence ever discovered my dreadful tracing habit, he'd have been sure to torture me but good. You see, air tracing the outlines of objects with my index finger had been my soothing and, up to then, secret compulsion. I'd trace most anything: barns, stagecoaches, trees. In church, I even surreptitiously traced the heads of the parishioners in the pews in front of me.

The Sunday Lawrence Walters disappeared, Reverend Ahern's sermon was about forgiveness. The whole while, all

I thought about was Lawrence and how I could never forgive him no matter what the Bible said. After church, I once again, snuck away to the old twisted oak tree, feeling compelled to trace all its nooks. With its scraggly gnarled branches, flaky gray bark, and thick twisted trunk, the tree looked how I felt, an odd stick that didn't belong.

I swear I spent a hundred hours air tracing the strange old tree that summer. And the more I traced it, the more I got an odd, almost indescribable feeling. Somehow, the air around the tree felt like a frozen lake in late winter, where you have to step gingerly, so as not to break through the melting ice. It felt like if I wasn't careful I just might crash through the air around that tree, into Lord knows what. The birds, bees and crickets must've sensed it too because they sang all around that hill but never seemed to make their way up to the tree.

After church that day, I sat by the tree, tracing amidst the thinness when I noticed near the tree's base, floating over the bark, like wavy fumes above a fire, a dark three-foot void in the air, a rip. I couldn't understand how the air might rip, yet there it was, plain as day, hanging over the trunk of that tree like a withering black sun in the sky. Whatever might be on the other side of that rip, I didn't fancy knowing. It certainly didn't look like any Pearly Gates I'd ever heard of. Scared it might be the opposite, I nearly ran off in terror.

Just then, Lawrence Walters came trudging up the hill. He'd caught me tracing, again. With his sickening sadistic smile and those dark soulless eyes, leering behind locks of stringy black hair, I knew what was coming. He reached into the pocket of his trousers, but before he could pull out a knife and cut off more of my hair, I pushed him, hard— right toward the base of the tree.

He fell backward. I don't rightly know if I meant to push him into that bizarre hole in the air. But mean it or not, I did it, and like some invisible toad catching a fly, the hole swallowed Lawrence Walters up. As he fell back, something dropped from his hand— something that stunned me just as much as his vanishing into... well, into thin air.

At the time, I didn't rightly know what happened. Years later, my best guess is that the fabric of our world was dangerously thin by that twisted old tree, and my air tracing must've been more than it could handle, a blade slicing through a worn canvas. After that incident, I stopped tracing the tree altogether, and the rip slowly mended, day-by-day, until by the end of the summer it disappeared completely, just like the boy it swallowed.

It's been seven years now since Lawrence Walters went missing, and I still have my blonde pigtail. The one he dropped before disappearing— braided and twisted into the shape of a heart.

CURT CLAPPER

Curt's Acknowledgments:

A personal note to you, our reader-

Writing is a trip the writer and reader embark on together. To amazing places, horrible places, reassuringly ordinary places. Ambling off. Coming home. Together, reader and writer.

Writing is a conversation, working our way toward truth. Or finding kindness. Showing us who we can...and who we want to be.

Writing amuses us, teaches us, warms us. Writing sparks ideas.

Writing lets us see the world through other eyes.

In writing we engage those gone and yet to come.

There are amazing people to meet. A.M. is joi de vivre. D.S. loves exploring. V.J. shows the way. D.V.S. and B.W. bring 'friend' into the real world. Writing helps me know them.

What an amazing universe: beautiful, terrible, filled with awe. Evolving galactic superstructures, myriad ecosystems, the microscopic formation and conduct of life. Organizing principles underlying everything. Life moving through every dimension of emotion, connection, or distance; love, hatred, change, death, creation. The reaches of being.

Writing connects us to these— and to each private realm of imagination.

Writing lets us touch the world, and what we touch we can change.

Writing changes us.

There is wonder here.

To explore together-
CURT CLAPPER

The Old Man, the Squirrels, the Birds, and the Chipmunks

by Curt Clapper

Once there was an old man with serious problems in his life. When he carefully considered his problems, though, he found them not particularly interesting, merely real. So he did what he could to resolve them, then turned his regard to the larger world that surrounded him.

One day, he stepped outside his door, dusted off the saucer from an old flowerpot, and filled it with seeds and nuts. He set this on the ground where wildlife would easily find it.

Squirrels discovered the saucer almost immediately. Birds appeared. Chipmunks scurried in, and dashed away.

The old man put out fresh seeds and nuts as each new sunrise flooded up into the stars. Through hard winters and scant springs, his saucer made a difference. As nights blossomed into dawns, more birdsong danced through the woods, even on bleak winter mornings.

More squirrels chased one another over frozen clattering winter branches, past delicate spring blossoms, through dark summer leafy shadows and into papery autumn leaves. Chipmunks erupted from the undergrowth more frequently and darted off, racing each other down minute green trails. Wings fluttered overhead. Movement shimmered everywhere: in trees, over stones and through the tall grasses.

At dawn, the birdsong was astonishing.

Sometimes, the old man would sit and watch. Cardinals and titmice swooped in. He began to recognize individual squirrels and their personalities. Once, two chipmunks burst into a joyful sortie from one secret niche to the next, and this struck him as an event. He began to see these wild lives as they changed and as their paths crossed. He began to notice moments in his own life. Everything became more interesting. Life grew intense. From time to time, he laughed.

Eventually the upturned saucer was left empty. The wild lives shifted once again into older patterns. Slowly, the birdsong diminished and there was less movement through the trees and tall grasses.

Spring showers and autumn leaves fell and tumbled away.

From time to time, a woman who lived down the lane remembered how the birds, in their tumultuous chorus, once welcomed dawn. Those memories warmed her, and she smiled. One day in the market, she became still, her head to one side, lost in thought. She stood for several moments, then added a quantity of nuts and seeds to her basket.

Days fly onward.

Moral: Do what you can, while you can.
You may change everything.

Spring

by Curt Clapper

What can I say?
The light will not come and curl up at my feet
as it did for someone it loved.

Spring leaves are lovely
but whisper only their affection for the breeze.

The moist turned earth is rich with tumult
but gives nowhere to stand.

The star that marks the pole
is fixed
but only on its own aspiration.

Each simple grass has its root
but—
where will I be?
What fit is there for me?

My hope is only that I am
the Commencement
ready to begin.

Note

by Curt Clapper

Nothing happens in general.
Everything happens in particular.

Haiku

by Curt Clapper

On a tatami
watching the snow with plum wine-
it is very sweet.

One

by Curt Clapper

Without reading
There is no writing.

Without writing
There is no reading.

In reading we begin to write.

Little Light

by Curt Clapper

Leaves are streaking from the trees. Wind pushes them into fluttering diagonals of orange and caramel confetti. Beautiful to see, driving past the park. But I have miles to go and groceries thawing in the back of the van. They need my refrigerator and I need to get them there.

Pulling into the garage. The van rear lift-gate swings almost (but not quite) to the ceiling of the garage. As always. Dozen brown bags to troop into the house, up the stairs, to the kitchen counter. Three treks up and down and up the stairs. Find the ice cream and the frozen pie. Find the frozen vegetables. Into the freezer. Milk and hot dog relish into the fridge. Hotdogs into the meat keeper. Dump trick-or-treats into our special basket. Then pantry boxes: cereal, pancake mix, tea. Bags stowed away.

I take the bars of soap and the little box with the new nightlight. Ferry them upstairs and down the hall to the kids' bathroom. Soap stowed. Night light popped from its box and plugged into the spare outlet over the sink. I should do a quick test. Shut the door on their windowless bathroom. Overhead light off. A second...and the new little luminescent panel springs to life: a pale, pleasant yellow glow. Like moonlight. Good. Done. Light on. Door open. Next chore.

Day is finally done. Organize the kids for bed. Little Tina, three years old, is too busy for bed: discovering a new game for Barbie in her own special world. Toby, six, is wrapped solidly in a picture book about dinosaurs. Both extracted, cajoled, commanded, and finally tickled into baths, pajamas, and beds. Nightly stories told. The lights turned down, covers tucked. Goodnight hugs and kisses. The last obligatory questions and responses, postponing the final stillness of the day as long as possible. At last it's done. The dinner dishes are in the sink and need attention. And then the house is dark. Up two flights to the attic and our master bedroom, the door left open as always. Reading: I can read two more chapters in my book... but fatigue is making my eyes difficult to control, hard to sweep across, along the page. Enough. Light off. Covers up. Sliding further under the comforter, then nothing exists. Nothing at all.

Tina is screaming. My foot hits the carpeting. Pounding down the stairs. Before I can even make the turn into the hallway, Toby is yelling "Daddy! Daddy!"

I round the corner into their hallway. Looks wrong. The nightlight in the hall is on, a pale little yellow glow. The bathroom door is ajar. But the light from the doorway— wrong. No bright overhead. No moonlight yellow. Pale green.

I know that green. Not here. It can't be here. I am tearing down the hall and I grab the edge of the bathroom doorway to swing myself in, instantly reaching to hit the overhead light. The overhead light floods the bathroom and the screaming stops instantly. Tina and Toby are staring into the wall of mirror, mouths agape. Tina has her hand pressing her forehead, Toby, his hands on his head, staring into the mirror.

"I bleeding!" Tina wails. I swing myself to sit on the toilet and pull her into my arms and onto my lap.

"Let me see, darling. Where does it hurt?"

"Daddy! Hair's gone!" Toby shouting.

I am gently pulling Tina's hand away from her forehead. There is no sign of blood, no smears, nothing dried; no injury I can see.

"My ow-ey, Daddy." She is looking at her hand. "My blood?" Her hand is clean, nothing on it. I can't see anything wrong. Hand. Forehead. All fine.

Toby is still looking into the mirror. "My hair's back! How'd you do that?" I am looking at my two kids, who are fine, who look just exactly the way they did when I tucked them in a few hours ago.

"What happened? What did you see?"

"I bleeding. On my head." says Tina, wrapping herself against me.

"My hair went away! All away!"

I don't know what to say. Ellie's traveling on business. Separation from Mom— anxiety, so bad dreams? I can't see anything wrong, though I am examining Tina's forehead and the top of her scalp. Toby has come over and has his arms around us both, wanting to be included in the hug. I put my arms around them both.

"It's okay. Everything's okay now. I know. Let's have a Family Campout in the big bedroom upstairs." Always a popular option. "We'll pile under the covers, okay? What story shall we read?"

"But Mommy's not here." Tina is mumbling into my pajama top.

"But she wants to be. And we'll have another Family Campout when she gets back, okay?"

"Can I bring Brownie?" Toby asks. Brownie is his teddy.

"Of course, Toby. Tina, do you want to bring Candy?" Her plush pink unicorn. She nods against the flannel of my pajamas.

"Ok, pumpkins. Go get your friends. Let's head upstairs!" They are gone in an instant.

I quickly scan the bathroom. Everything fine. No mold.

No twisted shelves of fungus springing from the walls. How?

Years ago Grandpa and I were tramping out across his farm late at night. That chill autumn night, under the stars, he spoke of constellations and the history of the hills. Then we climbed back, far up the mountain. Deep in the woods we came upon a huge oak brought down in a storm, trunk stretched along the ground, rotting between the trees still standing around it.

But its stump, shattered, sprouted broad fungus shelves, convoluted and fluorescing. Silent under the stars. Pale green luminescence oozing into the night, staining the darkness.

"Hate them things." He grabbed my jacket. "Keep away."

Fungus glow had been seeping out the bathroom door. Pale green fluorescence had been creeping out across our hallway carpet.

I reached quickly for the light switch. Off. A second of darkness. Then yellow moonlight as the nightlight glow comes on.

Overhead: On.

Off. Yellow moonlight.

I throw the overhead switch on as my two young ones bound into the doorway.

I smile.

"Ok, kids! Off to the Campout! Last one under the covers is a rotten egg!" Pounding up the stairs to the big bedroom upstairs.

Crazy night. But today has been good. Kids insisted on wearing their costumes all day. Just taking the pie out of the oven, putting it on top of the stove to cool, when I hear a series of bumps and Tina starts to wail. Out to the stairs—she is on the landing, sobbing, holding her forehead.

"What's wrong, honey? Did you fall? Can I see?"

She is nodding. I gently move her hands from her forehead. Her Princess crown is askew, one point has knocked her forehead, drawing blood. Gently lift it away. Doesn't look deep. She's already recovering from the shock and surprise; the wailing is subsiding into sniffles and she is rubbing her eyes.

"Come on, sweetheart. We'll go upstairs and clean up a little. I think you deserve a Princess band-aid. What do you think?" She is hugging me and nods, sniffling, against my shirt. I scoop her up and head upstairs.

In the bathroom I set her down and run warm water on a washcloth. Toby comes in, wearing his homemade Frankenstein costume: my old sport coat, my old jeans. While I wring out the washcloth, I realize they are both silent, staring into the mirror.

"Cool!" Toby says. "How'd you do that, Daddy?"

"What do you mean?"

"That's us. Last night!" I realize that he has on my bald wig from "The King And I". Tina has her hand on her forehead, touching the blood.

"Don't get your blood on your costume, honey." I pick her up and sit down on the toilet, begin to gently pat her forehead with the warm washcloth. I have already pulled out a band aid with pink crowns and stars, and she takes it, delicately unwrapping the sticky parts.

"Is that the right one for your costume?"

She is nodding yes, it is. Band-aid on, she likes her image in the mirror. Her Princess crown now covers most of the injury. Crisis past.

But something feels wrong. Way wrong.

Front door bell. Downstairs we all go.

Our next-door neighbor and her little girl. "Marcy! You brought a witch! Oh! It's Suzy! You scared me for a minute, Suzy!"

"Toby, show them what we have in our treats basket."

Marcy is going to take the kids out Trick-or-Treating while I listen for the other neighborhood kids to come by. And I have another project, too, while they're gone.

"Don't scare people too much, you two! The pumpkin pie is cooling off, and I'll have the ice cream ready when you get back!"

There've been no ghosts or goblins at the door for some time. I head upstairs to the bathroom. The overhead is on, everything looks right. Two fresh towels on the towel racks. Sink clean, counter clear. I look up at the overhead light, bright and steady. I hit the switch.

A moment of darkness. Then yellow moonlight from the luminescent nightlight.

Overhead on. Bright.

Overhead off. Moonlight.

On. Bright.

Off. Moonlight.

Bright.

Moonlight.

Bright.

Moonlight.

Bright.

Moonlight.

Bright.

Moonlight.

Bright.

Moonlight.

Bright.

Moonlight.

Fungus green. Everywhere. Pale in the darkness. Faint fluorescence. *Green.*

So dark in this pale glow. In the opposite wall of mirrors I see the bathroom faintly in darkness— a towel skewed on the rack. Other missing. Something messy covering the sink countertop— can't tell what.

In this faint green fluorescence there are no colors, only shapes. Can't understand. On the floor, over the little carpet, is more stuff, like on the sink. Everywhere. Big lumps in places. But in this faint fluorescence I can make out no colors.

Nothing makes sense in all this. What I see in my mirror, in the green florescence just makes no sense. In this glowing, nothing that makes sense-

Overhead: on. Bright.

Towels in place. Nothing on the counter.

Clean fluffy rug on the floor.

Marcy –

Leaving this note on front door because we have a problem here. Do NOT come in. Ring bell. If I don't come, please take kids home with you? Will bring pie– Be there soon as possible.

When you get home could you call police and ask them to check our house? Door is unlock

Oh God. Lights went out. The lights are out. Just the little emergency light under the kitchen cabinets above the kitchen counter.

From my kitchen island I should see three neighbors' houses through the big windows. But now there is nothing. There is nothing outside the windows. Absolutely nothing. Solid blackness pressing on the glass.

So quiet. Oh God. It's getting cold. Air is moving-

Arctic air is moving through the house.

It can't get this cold. Not this fast. Not inside. See my breath. I'm freezing.

Something bad is happening – can't understa

Frost is creeping across the stone countertop toward me.

Oh God Ellie I Love you. Forever

Tell Toby and Tina I Love them

Every Day- Always

Toby. Tina. Oh *God*.
Coming. Here. In all this

Upstairs-
something falls

Silence

Breath freezing in air

Stillness

Freezing

Oh God Ellie I am going upstairs to
see what is in the bathroom

JIM ELGAS

Jim's Acknowledgements:

Watertown, West Allis... Route 66... Dallas, Fort Worth... Route 66... Hollywood, Pasadena, South Pasadena, El Monte, Glendora, Orange, Laguna Beach... Route 1... San Francisco, Chico... Pacific Ocean... Caribbean, Virgin Gorda, Canada, Vancouver Island, Banff, Quebec... back and forth... Traveling... North and South... East and West... Bridgewater, Vermont... Key West... box-cars... making music... reading... flatcars... semis... hitchhiking... walking... laughing... praying... being one of ten kids... writing... dreaming... Todos Santos... Santa Fe... Arlington Heights, etc... to be continued...

Acknowledgements: to the Creator... to all those who have taught me how to live and share through example... Twain, Dylan, Prine, Earle, Jennings, Mom, Dad, Spider, Savage, Joe, The Professor, Donnie, Forbidden Jimmy, Larry & the Road Angels (not enough space in any book to name)... to all those who have gone... to our past & present pets- Duke, Cody Rose, Gabby, Lucky, Beau... and to the greatest gifts of all... Mindy and Kelsey... my reasons for living.

JIM ELGAS

The Cold Trail

(A Burlesque Biography)

by Jim Elgas

Back in the days of begetting there were no last names. So tracing ancestry to ancient times is impossible for most, but for myself, the task is easier. Fortunately, the earliest of my lineage were educated and well-versed in the fine arts of semantics and vernacular.

Amos the Ancient, my first recorded family member, appeared on the scene shortly after the Great Flood. He was listed on the Ark's log as one of the original boat people and was a noted Scrabble player in Noah's inner circle. His constant play on words led him to concocting last names for individual families. Why did he choose "Elgas" for himself? Yahweh only knows! Word has come down that he thought it poetic when coupled with his first name.

Appropriately, my ancestral trail picks up again in the village of Babel, where semantics played another major role. The fruit never falls far from the tree, or in this case, the tower. It is here we find the next branch in my family history- Jobab Elgas.

Jobab married Jo-mama, who was a direct descendant of Cush and Nimrod, co-founders and property barons of the Village of Babel in the Land of Shinar.

Jobab never got on the bandwagon for the grand scale development that took place in Babel. In fact, in good conscience, he opposed it. His way with words carried him to the general assembly where he lobbied tirelessly as a voice of the people who didn't, or couldn't care less to speak up. But as is the case, the expansion zealots won out and eventually brought about the downfall of Babel. Their public rhetoric so baffled the general populace that nobody knew who was for what, and what was for who. Seeing the end in sight, Jobab and Jo-mama fled and settled in the Land of Nod, 20 miles east of Eden.

Fast forwarding through the next three millennia, we leave many less noble family members in our wake. Less noble because they never subscribed to the high ideals of being snuffed out for something that others believed in. Some say they were actually on a loftier plane than the higher-minded side of the Elgas clan.

Among them was Barrabbas Elgas, the leader of a band of chicken thieves who plundered the private estates of Roman prelates in the thunderous times of the Messiah. His catch phrase, "A chicken in every hovel," never really caught on. Though later, in modern times, a politician revived the line with a slightly different slant. Unfortunately, he roused about the same amount of enthusiasm as Barrabbas.

Then there was Cheat-cha-boo Elgas, the court jester for King Richard. He exuded the lighter side of life, and was considered so ahead of his time that he didn't even know what he was talking about!

Later came Coma-toma-homa-bomba Elgas, or "The Lounge Lizard," as his father called him. Coma was the last born in a family of 10. He had been so doted on and catered to, as a child, that he grew up thinking the rest of mankind owed him a living. The stick-to-it-tivness of his belief finally paid off when he was awarded, by local authorities, a lifetime admission pass for three hots and a cot at a "males only" institution.

I will mention, in passing, my great-grandfather, Braggadocio Elgas. He was a beat cop from a small Midwest town who met his untimely end while relieving himself on high-voltage power lines from the roof of the local police precinct building. The family has been in shock ever since.

I will not pass comment on the history of my father, because I'm still on speaking terms with him.

Arriving at the present, I will now shed light on my own private blip on the eternity screen. I was born with webbed toes and a wanderer's heart. Dreams have always played a major role in my survival, and with any luck they will continue. The rest of the story can't be told because it hasn't taken place yet.

Huckleberry Hubris

by Jim Elgas

You don't know about me lessen' you have read some shawt stories from da past in dis heah almanak. Dey was written by a Mr. Jim Elgas, who tells da truth mainly. To be sure he stretches sumthings sumtimes but dats jes to prove a pint and to paint a mo akrit pitchur. It's no big deal. Why, dere ain't one amongst us who hasn't lied at one time or anutha and if'n anyone begs ta differ wid dat, well den, dey shudn't be trusted ta begin wid!

Anyways, me and Mr. Elgas haz been frends for a long time, same side of da traks so to speak. We'b had many conversayshuns but mostly I end up doin all da talkin'. Dat suits him fine and he don't mind. He's a good listener and enjoys da sermons.

Da way he puts it is dat, "everybodys got a gift and should be obliged ta use it." He says dat mine jes happens to be "common sense" and my uncanny way of espressin it. He adds dat accordin' ta hiz observashun, it haz not been properly distribuhted amongst da masses.

I told him dat in mah opinion common sense has takin' a back seat to pursonal ajendas. And wen dat happens and offends da innocent, why, I can't help mysef. I become a virtual volcano of vernackular and a frend to da defenceless. It's only natchural and I don't hinder its intrusion. I cant help it if'n dats da way I wuz made!

To be sure ah've received mah fair share of ire and retaliation but dat don't botha me none, I don't hav much ta lose. Anyways, I know da diffrence between right an wrong. And jes becauze dem dat perpetuate da wrong mite be educated and hold sway in dis heah world, it still don't hold no water wid me if'n dey are takin advantige of dem dat arn't. Education is a privilege and should not be used against dem dat don't hold dat same privilege You'da thought dey mite know bettah!

In mah view mos of todays problems find der sources in money and powah and dem dat seeks em. Oh dey can skewah da most sacrid and revered truths and twis dem ta make it look like da Almighty himsef wuz on der side. But I ask ya, "wouldn't it be bettah if dey wuz on his side?

Bear wid me, I hav a tendency to wanda but der are so many things to discuss and so little space to put dem in.

For instance, I git a lot a people askin me about mah name and where't comes from. Well, if'n you look in da dictionary you'll find a curious thing. In it, you'll see dere's a definition for both of mah names and dey are right next to each other. Of coarse Hubris appeahs first, which is only propah, cause dats where mos of mah views come from. It's an old handle dat dates back to da fall ov man in da gawden and originally was da name of one of da first trees dere. Frankly, I think we all share a bit of ancestry in da roots of dat old tree, but for me it jes happens to be mah moniker and I suppose ma downfall in da long run. As for mah first name mah mama luved dat fruited shrub and dats good enuff fer me.

As you can probably tell I'm not an educated man in a societal sense, but I hav learned to read. I know dat in mah head I hav writtin' the great American short story a 1,000 times but nevah on paypah. It's jes not mah gift. So Mr. Elgas has taken it upon hisself to part da waters wid mah conclusions. It's true he haz never used mah name in his storys but I do recognize da voice in hiz characters and appreciate da platform. Why once he even placed my orations in da mouth of a woman! ...Whatevah gits da message out I say.

Now I don't bow down to no sacred cows but mus admit dey do make da best burgers. I'm appalled by da pandered rhetoric of dose who happen to be in authority and use dere position fer deception. Why, we could heat da homes of all da poor if'n anyone could figga out a way to harness da blasts of hot air from dem blowhards. But dey will hav der own rewards. Bye and bye der undeserved accolades and self-appointed titles will be appropriately etched on der headstones and forgotten as quickly as dah selfserving lives dah've led.

I hope I don't appeah to harsh in mah outpourings. Mah mood is light mos of da time and besides I'm still welcomed in da company of old dogs and chillun. Instinctual I guess.

To sum things up, we live in a world of misinfurmashun and mos people don't hav da time or inclination to sort things out. But da sortin out will come in its own appointed time. Besides, dat bizness belongs to da source of all wizdum and I reckon' He's got a plan. Anyways, we've all got our own bizness to attend to and Lord knows dat deres enuff to fill each day!

Notice!

People attempting to find a motive in this narrative should examine their own; those attempting to find a moral in it shall be rewarded; those attempting to find a political agenda should seek a new profession.

BY ORDER OF THE AUTHOR
(CHIEF OF FIREARMS)

Dedicated to my friend, Vern Witcher

A Day in the Life of Jake Sellers, River Raft Pilot on the Styx

(A Warm Tale for a Winter's Night)

by Jim Elgas

It seemed a little steamier than normal in Hades. Jake knew this could mean only one thing. The "new shades," or recent arrivals, would be of a caliber who justly deserved their impending final rewards. It was a tradition of the welcoming committee to turn up the heat for just such occasions.

Jake's presence here, along with his duties, involved unusual circumstances. It seems there was an erroneous mix-up of his paperwork after his earthly demise. He had accidentally been sent to this destination, which was in direct contrast to his worldly achievements and actions. And sadly, due to the laws of the Almighty, which are final, this oversight could not be undone.

But it didn't bother Jake much. He was accustomed to injustice, having served his time as a human. So in compensation he was appointed to the position of raft pilot to ferry the lost souls over the Styx River through the nine rings circling the parameters of Hell.

Now, one might wonder what a pilot should say to those arriving at the gates of damnation. Is there an appropriate greeting surrounding the gravity of such an event?

Being a humorous soul, Jake concocted what might be the simplest icebreaker imaginable.

"Hell-O!" he spouted, with as much enthusiasm as was proper. But his jest was lost on the three new shades who were preoccupied with their foreboding eternal future at hand.

By and by, their previous lives revealed themselves as Jake poled out to reach the molten current of the River Styx.

"I insist on a fair and balanced account on the details of my final destination," demanded the former editor of a national newspaper chain.

"Well," said Jake, "according to the Associated Press Release of Hell, you are destined to a spot near Zone 2 in the ninth and innermost circle of Hades, where you will spend eternity running in opposite directions from yourself."

"Hold on a minute!" snapped the editor. "Are you implying that I was a fence-sitter on Earth and never took a stand on any vital issues?"

"Not at all," said Jake, "I'm just parroting the limited news resources available to us in the hereafter." The editor then realized that the similarities between his earthly practice of controlled reporting from government sources and those of Hell were one and the same, and yes, *slightly* biased. So he fell silent and accepted his fate.

After a period of unspecified time, which seemed an eternity, the second of the threesome, a CEO of an international oil company, inquired of what his destiny dictated.

Jake didn't know precisely, but again referred to the report. "I see here that you are to be spirited, on an alternating basis, between three districts forever. The first being District 3 where you'll be forced to drink the product you exploited and hoarded on Earth. In the second one, or District 4, you'll be expected to transfer that same product, from tanker to tanker, using only a spoon. And lastly, you'll make regular appearances to the inner ring of Circle 7 and be put in charge of dispersing umbrellas during firestorms." He then added, "And according to other shades in similar situations, you'll come to appreciate the diversity."

"Hell-a-cious," muttered the CEO as reality set in.

The last passenger, a corrupt pocket politician, who possessed the ancient rhetoric of Babel, began offering up his sincerest regrets for his misguided life as a public servant in pursuit of private graft. And then returning to character added... "What's in it for me?"

Jake sighed deeply and began, "According to the chart, you are to be ferried to a newly created zone within the ninth circle. Upon entry, you will be stuffed upside down in a pocket of echoes and forced to listen to all of your earthly public orations and inane policy positions, all of which were motivated by greedy self-interest."

The politician stood motionless, looking like he never comprehended a word, and then blurted out; "Well what's so bad about that?"

"That's the Hell of it, sir," said Jake, "and you won't know the suffering until you get there!"

Snapshots
from the Other Side

by Jim Elgas

Homelessness is a dark reminder of a flawed society. It is dignity stripped bare, but need not be a dead end to optimism.

Unfortunately, dignity is not a birthright. It is possessed by those who are content with their circumstances and can be passed along by simple respect for one another. It is, after all, not pity that the homeless want, but merely our acknowledgement of them as fellow human beings. The following tales are of two individuals whose lifestyles are at odds with the prevailing societal judgments of the homeless.

Snapshot #1: "Vilas Bridge"

Vilas Bridge is a native Vermonter with family ties dating back to its statehood. When I knew him, he was around 60 years of age, long-haired, bearded, and shabbily dressed. His education consisted of what he had learned while growing up in the backwoods of the Green Mountains.

During the winter months, in exchange for his sidewalk snow shoveling, the shire town of Woodstock, Vermont, allowed him to sleep in the basement of an old theater building. In the summer, he would sweep the same sidewalks, but preferred to set up his abode beneath one of the fabled covered bridges along the Ottaquechee River. I met and would see him often on the village green in the center of town where he was somewhat of a tourist attraction. Being a true character and link to Vermont's colorful past, visitors wanted their picture taken with him. He would oblige them for a small fee of one dollar.

When business was slow, he would return to panhandling from the locals. I'd always give him whatever change I had in my pockets, but once he surprised me when I told him I didn't have any. He looked me in the eye and said, "I got money, you need some?" He proceeded to show me an old bankbook, from a neighboring town, with his name on it. As it turned out, he had more capital than I did. I asked him why he didn't use a local bank instead. He said because it would be too easy to get to and might defeat the purpose of saving to begin with. So much for the village-idiot opinion held by the locals.

From time to time, he'd corner me into driving him some-where to see something he considered wild and wonderful. One time, it was to show me where the purest water in all of Vermont was to be found. After tasting it I became a believer, although I confess I had a moment of trepidation after seeing the "Contaminated- Do Not Drink" sign next to the spring. He assured me that whoever had posted the notice wanted it all to himself. And besides, I'm still here.

Another adventure involved the whereabouts of the biggest squash grown in all of New England. After 10 miles of back-road driving, we came upon an old overgrown crop plot which, by all appearances, may have been originally cultivated by the first settlers. And there lying in the dirt were huge squash, some eight feet long.

"Okay," I said, "but aren't the smaller ones tastier?"

"Yes, indeed," he said, "but I didn't take you to see the best tasting ones, though I know where they are, too!"

When we moved from Vermont, the last person I saw

as we were driving out of town was old Vilas sweeping the sidewalks.

Snapshot #2: "Rudy from the Baja"

My second tale involves an excursion to the enchanting southern Baja Peninsula of Mexico, and the then-sleepy fishing village of Todos Santos (All Saints). The subject is another homeless man, named Rudy, who was the first contact I had made during my stay.

The first morning there, I awoke to a pristine sunrise and immediately set out to find a cup of coffee. Walking in the same direction, but on the other side of the street, I spied a middle-aged man whistling in harmony with the birds of daybreak. He strolled along with the carefree walk of a child in Eden, carrying a dusty old gunnysack filled with who knows what.

"Hola, mi amigo!" he shouted in my direction.

Having the paranoia of a cautious tourist, I looked around and noticed there was no one else about. So I returned an "Hola!" to him. He took it as an invitation to join me and started right in on a Spanish oration that could only have been about the beauty of the day. All the while his hands waved expressively while pointing out the bougainvillea and jasmine flowers draping the adobe walls. The sunrise, I'm certain, was mentioned at some point in his sermon, though I understood little of the Spanish he spoke. Instant amigos were we, and I felt welcomed in his presence.

During my stay, I would see him now and then in unexpected places. His spirit would bring a heightened sense of life to each of our encounters.

Once, on a deserted beach miles from town, he appeared like a mirage on the shore. Behind him surfaced some California gray whales with their babies, and above the sound of the surf, I heard the familiar "Hola, amigo!"

Another time, on a street corner, I saw him feeding stray dogs from his burlap bag. Each was given a butcher bone or bread crumbs. They crowded around him like the return of the Messiah... he called them "amigos" also.

Then there was the chance meeting on the patio of the Lingusta Loco Restaurant. I welcomed him to our table, but felt the uneasiness of the owners and his reluctance to accept my invitation. I ordered him a drink anyway and noticed tears welling in his eyes at my gesture of friendship. He amigo'd me to the last drop of his drink and then rummaged through his sack, pulling out a solid silver medal with the image of a swordfish.

"For you, mi amigo," he said.

The morning I left Todos Santos, I walked the streets looking for Rudy, but he was nowhere to be found. Then as I drove out to the edge of town, I saw him sweeping the gutters with a broom. I pulled over and got out to give him a hug. In broken English, hardly discernible, he expressed his thanks for my friendship, and if I'm not mistaken, made me promise to bring him a color television when I returned.

I'm often reminded of these two human beings, but more so now as I sit in our local library, surrounded by the homeless with the holiday season fast approaching...

Going, Going...

by Jim Elgas

"Daddy! Come git me. It's 16 o'clock!" These were not the earliest words or memories I have of my then two year old daughter but they've stuck to my brain like the applesauce use to stick to her chin at high chair meals.

These words came early each morning from her crib. She was usually up with the birds and singing too. This habit changed though when she learned to scale her confines. Thereafter, the first sounds would be that of her small-socked feet beating a path from her room to ours and ending with a silent leap onto her prone and unprotected father. I've been covering up, when kids are present, ever since!

She was always on the go. "Let's go to the park!" "Let's go swimming!" "Let's go to the store!" "Let's go play!" And when there was no destination in mind, it was just, "Let's go!"

I also remember her as a 3-year-old break dancing at a Vermont ski-lodge and how everyone else stopped to form a circle and clap.

I remember the "Daddy Song" she made up for me. I had to laugh to keep from crying.

Children have an innate sense of innocent wisdom if one would stop and listen. Once on a remote beach in Baja Mexico, she looked up and spotted a white gull floating motionless overhead. I told her what type of bird it was, hoping to impart some human knowledge. She looked back to me and responded, "That's where the Spirit of God lives." So much for my earthly details…

We traveled a lot while she was small. When we finally settled she was almost five and ready for school. I remember her first day. She was so excited that she didn't have time for us to take a posed picture. So the shot we have of her is walking up the sidewalk with body half turned and waving. Going, going…

In the elementary school years our connection was strong. During this time she would still cuddle on the recliner, give me hugs, and depend on my assistance. But the, "Daddy come git me" phrase was revised to, "Daddy go git me." It ran the range from, "git me some ice cream" to, "git me some clothes", then to, "git me some make-up" and finally, "git me a car!" About the only time the old "Daddy come git me" adage was used, at this stage, was to go and pick her up from the movies but it was now joined with, "and meet me two blocks away."

Things change when a child approaches the teen years. Their need for independence and the urge to distance themselves from their parents arrives with the subtleness of a thunderbolt to the heart. The pain is indescribable but part of the process.

The fun-loving Dad who once could make his daughter laugh without trying becomes the lame over-achieving clown who should not be encouraged. It's hard to accept the fact that, to her, you're now about as funny as Mr. Rogers trying to imitate George Carlin.

Then came the boys! If anything shakes up a father's vigilance for his daughter more than this, I don't want to experience it. This parade had quite a cast. Some showed up wearing the grunge look with pant legs long enough to trip men on stilts. There was one distant soul whose conversation and vocabulary consisted of two words, "Hell-low." It would have been difficult for me to beat an "ouch" out of him with a bat, yet the thought was tempting... But I digress!

This brings me to the reality of the June graduation date staring at me from the calendar. I find myself confronted with the soon to be sadness of separation which my wife had warned me about for years. Now, the memories flood back and I wonder if my daughter will recall them like I do.

I'll miss our many discussions on injustice and how she gave me the opportunity to rediscover my opinions by revealing hers. We really don't have any idea of what our views are until we raise a child because by then they're all put on trial.

I'm going to miss her presence most but there are many other things that have surfaced recently which are both comical and sad. I'm going to miss her relationship with our dog. She is an only child and our pet became her sibling. Thank God dogs don't speak the language!

I'll miss my bathroom radio disappearing and the dial-up computer line we shared. Okay, maybe I won't miss the shared line.

I'll miss the times we really laughed and the fact that she asked my advice for her essays.

I'll miss telling her that many of the songs she likes now are actually re-makes of the ones that I liked when I was her age.

I'll miss sitting up late, in the living room, with the T.V. on so she could fall asleep in her room.

I'll miss trying to give her the common sense I learned from experience so she might not have to make the same mistakes or suffer the consequences I did.

I'll miss her eyes because they are the same eyes of my mother and my mother's mother and they are both no longer with us.

She's not gone yet, but she'll be going, going... soon, and I'm going to miss her very, very much...

I Know, I Know!

by Jim Elgas

Wednesdays are usually uneventful days for most of us. Aside from its nickname of, "Hump Day," for being sandwiched between weekends, there's not much to get excited about. But for Mona Madden and Sara Shyrok, two stay-at-home Moms and lifelong friends, their Wednesdays were special like Sundays are to priests, or Fridays are to hard-working construction laborers. For Wednesday was their day to spend time together and catch up on the week.

Their lives had been linked since childhood. They'd grown up together in a lower middle-class neighborhood within an affluent community and suffered slight inferiority complexes because of it. Their parents were close friends and they each had a younger brother. Right out of college, both had married doctors and given birth to daughters within the same year.

Personality-wise they were opposites, as most close relationships require. Mona Madden was the outspoken one, with opinions on everything. Her beliefs were the by-products of her emotions, which were gleaned from the shallow pools of gossip columns, entertainment magazines, and quick glances at front page headlines. Talking came easy for Mona, but often took no particular direction. Her topics jumped from one to another with hardly a breath in-between. She'd hate to admit it, but she was a carbon copy of her mother, a woman with a good heart, but who was personally frustrated with her lot in life.

On the other hand, her friend, Sara Shyrok, was quiet and preoccupied. A wallflower with ears. She never could express her feelings and was content to stand in Mona's shadow, nodding in agreement whether she shared the same opinion or not. Their interactions weren't too dissimilar from the relationship of her parents. Her passivity gave the impression of inner peace, but for Sara, it was only a veil to conceal her imagined inadequacies. Self-confidence wasn't her strong suit.

On this Wednesday, in mid July, they chose a deserted beach along Lake Michigan. With their 7-year-old daughters in tow, they found a flat spot and laid out their blankets. The girls grabbed their beach toys and ran off to build sandcastles by the water, while staying within earshot of their moms. As usual, Mona was armed with her peeves of the week, and before Sara could lie down, the oration began.

"I've been thinking about snobby people. They're every-where! Rich snobs, status snobs, political snobs, my family lived here longer than your family snobs, SUV snobs, punk snobs, and even homeless snobs. You name 'em, we've got 'em. I bet there's even an anti-snob snob among us," she said unloading her first volley.

"I know, I know," Sara agreed.

"While everyone is so busy overachieving to stay 'one-up' on whomever they're trying to impress, humanity has taken a backseat in a car with no driver," Mona went on.

"Busy, busy, busy! It's like a continuous distraction, keeping everyone's focus on something other than reality. Got to pay the mortgage. Got to pay the gas, water, and electric bills. Got to pay the life insurance in case you work yourself to death. And don't forget your car, boat, and new room additions, along with saving for your kid's college tuition, and oh yes, we've got to pay our taxes!

"There's the gas tax, the property tax, food taxes, the business tax, the state tax, the social security tax, the federal income tax, tolls, and my favorites, the sin taxes. AND NOW, our state government claims we have a deficit in our budget," Mona said with exasperation ringing in her words.

"I know, I know," Sara murmured apathetically.

"I guess it's easier for them to blame it on a sluggish economy, due to the overall belt tightening since the recession began, than to take fiscal responsibility for their own spending sprees. Their solution is to make budget cuts affecting our senior citizens, the needy, and the sick. They'll make sure they don't touch the pork used for government contracts that benefit their constituents who donate funds to their party's campaign re-election bids though. Tough decisions, indeed!" Mona said while turning blue from oxygen deficiency.

"Oh I know, I know," said Sara sounding almost interested.

"And getting back to snobs," Mona went on, "did I forget to mention the parent snobs? You know, the ones who are always raving about how smart their kids are, or what great athletes they've become. And what about the over-protective parent snobs, like Sally Shield? She's gotten so bad that she made her son wear a parka and ski pants in July so he wouldn't catch the West Nile virus. And what about the..."

A few yards away, Mona's daughter gave up on instructing Sara's little girl in the fine art of making sand castles. Instead, she started talking. "Aren't parents strange about every little thing? They go on and on and on and never stop. I can't believe it. It's such a pain to have to listen to them over and over, again and again. Isn't it?" she asked.

"I know, I know," answered Sara's little girl half-heartedly.

The 100 Million Dollar "LIFESTAKES" Handicap

by Jim Elgas

Part I - The Fanfare

Everyone who thought they were anyone was there, including myself and one stranger from Hannibal, Missouri, wearing his trademark three-piece white suit. He was known only to a small circle of friends as M.T. and had a double entry going that day in the biggest race of horse racing history.

It was opening day, a much anticipated event. "The Track was Back" and she never looked finer. "Horse Heaven," some proclaimed, "A Cruise Ship on Land," crooned others. But all the homage was mere chirping compared to her actual physical splendor. Like a jewel polished and buffed to a shine that was blinding. All attendants were dressed in such natty attire, that you couldn't tell the floor sweepers from the $1,000 minimum bet tellers. Everything was washed and scrubbed from the awning rafters to the cracks in the marble-tiled floors. All this and the sweet smell of May's lilac blooms wafting in the breeze. No matter who you were, high or low, rich or poor, you felt first-class. But I must return to the heart of the story. For now it was post time for the feature race and the 100 million dollars at stake.

Part II - The Entries

1 and 1/8 mile:

The Double Entry, #1 *Death* and #1A *Taxes*, were both owned by the aforementioned M.T. and were listed at 40-1 odds.

The #2 horse, *Corporate Takeover*, was owned by Fat Cat Enterprises out of New York City and was the 5-2 favorite.

Horse #3 *Perseverance* was owned by a partnership of ten struggling small business merchants. 30-1 odds.

Next up, the #4 horse, *Me First*, was owned by a self-proclaimed philanthropist who entered for the prestige. Going off at 3-1.

Then came #5, *Traffic Flow*, who was owned by a high official from the Illinois Road Commissioner's office. 10-1 odds.

Followed by #6, *Street Shadows*, who was owned and trained by a millionaire steel magnate at 20-1.

Up next #7, *Out of Focus*, owned by some newspaper chain. 9-2 odds.

Then the #8 horse, *Runway 32-L*, was owned by the Ay Carumba Paving Company. 12-1 odds.

Horse #9, *Go It Alone*, was owned by a local outspoken eccentric. 50-1 odds.

And finally the #10 horse, *Damage Control*, who was owned by the publisher of a magazine known as "that little yellow book." 99-1 odds.

The purse breakdown was divided in this manner: The winner takes home 50 million; the second horse receives 25 million; 3rd place 15 million; and the fourth horse 10 million.

Back on the track, the horses were loaded into the gates and tension mounted. Then, like a senior officer's "ATTENTION!" command, all the owners, except for M.T., whipped out cigars in unison, lit up and began puffing.

Part III - The Race

"AND THEY'RE OFF!" screamed the track announcer in a cracked voice inflicted with the anxiety surrounding the spectacle.

The horses leapt from the gates. Their hooves left craters the size of cooking woks. By the time the whip-lashed jockeys sprung back in their saddles, the horses had plotted their course and were bee-lining for early position on the rail. The inside double entry horses, *Death* and *Taxes*, were pinched back by the onslaught but didn't appear to be fazed. They settled into a comfortable gallop with both jockeys standing in their stirrups.

Meanwhile, at the head of the stampede, the fury continued. Horse legs and jockey whips flailed away trying to get an edge-up on the rest of the pack. Approaching the backstretch, *Corporate Takeover* and *Me First* muscled their way to the front and took turns leading with each stride. *Perseverance* hung tough and kept pace, one length back, all the way to the far turn.

Then it happened. The rest of the field suddenly remembered what was at stake and staged a cavalry charge on the leaders. All of them, that is except for *Death* and *Taxes*, who sauntered along ten lengths back, admiring the willow trees at the end of the backstretch.

When the herd rounded the far turn, they knotted up like cattle at a slaughterhouse. In desperation, those trailing the leaders were pulled outside by their jockeys to look for racing room. They fanned out across the track perpendicular to the rail.

"AND DOWN THE STRETCH THEY COME!" hollered the

announcer at the top of his lungs.

All the marbles were on the line as they entered the stretch. The nine other owners sprung to their feet with raised hands clutching racing forms. Though each of their horses were tied for the lead with a possible victory for any one of them, their eyes turned to the whirlwind whipping up three lengths back and gaining. What they saw was *Death* and *Taxes* closing like Siamese banshees joined at the hip. The roaring crescendo of the crowd grew an octave with their every stride.

M.T. rose slowly, and in a glance he measured the distance between his horses and the finish line. Then he gracefully ambled off in the direction of the Winner's Circle.

Back on the track, all the horses hit the wire simultaneously. The nine owners stood transfixed and dumb-founded. Nine cigars fell from their mouths like trees in a forest and no one noticed. The tote board lit up before the end of the race:

"PHOTO FINISH!"

Time froze on this spectacular May day. Later, some swore they heard the heartbeats of the owners as they hustled down to the Winner's Circle, petitioning the Gods they believed in.

Part IV - The Outcome

The stewards labored over the photos in what seemed an eternity.

"Too close to call," "Can't split `em," muttered voices in the multitude.

Then all at once the track announcer blurted out, "We have a Dead Heat! The winners are...

"Death and Taxes!"

There were muffled chuckles throughout the crowd, like the ones you hear after a bad pun, and they were amplified by the overflow of those in attendance.

The #3 horse, *Perseverance*, was declared the runner-up by a nose hair, and brought the ten small-business owners back from oblivion.

The #9 horse, *Go It Alone*, came in third. His outspoken owner immediately vowed to keep on speaking the truth.

And somehow the #10 horse, *Damage Control*, overcame the #7 horse, *Out of Focus*, and put his publisher-owner in the black.

There was madness in the Winner's Circle. It was so packed with people that the rails nearly collapsed. Photographers clicked away from every angle. Reporters clamored about trying to get close enough to interview the winning owner. When they finally reached him, one reporter thrust a microphone up to his bushy mustache and asked, "What made you decide to enter both of your horses in the same race?"

"Well," M.T. said slowly while drawing on his hand-rolled cigar, "It seemed like a sure thing to me."

And with that, I walked off to cash my two-dollar ticket on the winner.

Alienation Re-defined

by Jim Elgas

"How did it come to this?" thought the middle aged, mid-westerner Charley Mitty as he stared transfixed at the gaping excavation known as ground zero in lower Manhattan. Six years of soul numbing disbelief, six years of restless sleep, listening for anything new from the late night television talking heads and their continuous debate of the pros and cons of going to war with or without justification. In short, six years of contradictions.

Meanwhile, Charley mused, our basic rights are vanishing under the catch phrase of *Homeland Security*. The outsourcing of jobs is ratcheting up in earnest. The invasion of our privacy, now the norm, is looming with the imminent threat of chaos on every street corner of every town. And periodically we are presented with our very own terror alert meter to remind us of just how frightened we should be.

Charley contemplated these sobering realities as he eyed the passing strangers on the sidewalks of New York. With heads bowed, the crowds plodded by with no acknowledgement of one another. His thoughts drifted back to the days just prior to the decision to go to war. Any opposition to the proposed pre-emptive strike was being labeled as unpatriotic. Charley remembered one independent shop owner from his home town who, bravely stood up and opposed the plans.

One morning this man and his wife appeared on the platform of the local train station with signs protesting sending our troops to Iraq since no verifiable evidence had been presented proving their complicity in the 9-11 tragedy.

Largely their efforts were ignored by the non-interested commuter crowd. And they were only afforded the obligatory paragraph in the next day's news, conveniently buried on the back pages. Charley pulled himself from the memory and stepped off the curb to hail a cab.

"Times Square," he requested upon entering the caged back seat. Conversation was mute and the only communication between him and the cabbie was an occasional glance in the rear view mirror from a set of dark, heavy lidded eyes.

The license on the visor read, Kamil Al-Hakim. "Ironic," thought Charley as he feigned interest in the passing buildings outside his window.

Upon reaching his destination, Charley paid the fare and added a $20 dollar bill for the driver. "For your family" he said, not knowing if his words or intentions were even understood.

It was dark now and the lights of Times Square seemed as dim as the demeanors of the tourists he joined on the concrete. A maze of digital billboards shone down begging for attention from the preoccupied masses of iPod introverts and cell phone extroverts.

Feeling more isolated with each step, Charley snapped out of it when he caught sight of the iconic scrolling news board in the center of Times Square. The first message he eyed read:

...THE BAD NEWS IS...THERE IS NO GOOD NEWS...AND THE GOOD NEWS IS...WE'RE NOT GOING TO TELL YOU ABOUT THE BAD NEWS...

"Huh!" thought Charley, "A wise guy on the keyboard." The sign shot back:

...NOT SO CHARLEY...NOBODY IS PAYING ANY ATTENTION

ANYWAY...AS A MATTER OF FACT...MANY OF THE PEOPLE AROUND YOU CAN'T EVEN SPEAK ENGLISH...MUCH LESS READ IT...AND THE REST...AS YOU CAN SEE...ARE "HOOKED UP" AS THEY SAY...

"What the!" Charley gasped, "Are you talkin' to me?"

The message board flashed again:

...MAN CAUGHT ON CAMERA ACTUALLY READING MESSAGES IN TIMES SQUARE!...

Charley quickly looked around to see if anyone else was reading the postings. When his eyes returned to the board he caught sight of a huge Panasonic digital screen with a close up of himself looking bewildered and statue-like. "Very funny" Charley thought as he continued to read on.

...LATEST FINDINGS SHOW THAT SOME IMMIGRANTS ARE NOW LEAVING THE U.S. FOR BETTER ECONOMIC PROSPECTS IN DEVELOPING COUNTRIES...

"What next?" asked Charley to himself.

...IN THE FUTURE...THE NOW SHRINKING MIDDLE CLASS WILL CONSIDER IT A BLESSING TO BE EMPLOYED BY WALMART...

"Now that's far-fetched," said Charley, "or is it?"

...THERE'S MORE...REPORTS CONFIRM THAT AMERICANS ARE FALLING BEHIND ECONOMICALLY BY CONTINUING TO ELECT LEADERS WITH NO VISION FOR COMPETING IN THE TRANSITIONING GLOBAL MARKET...

"Well that strikes a chord," agreed Charley who was now totally engaged with each message.

...DUE TO THE UNABATED NEWS STORIES OF LINDSAY LOHAN AND THE AMERICAN IDOL TELEVISION PROGRAM ETC...ETC...MOST OF THE GENERAL PUBLIC HAVE BECOME NUMB AND COMPLETELY

UNINFORMED OF WHAT'S GOING ON IN THE WORLD...AMERICANS ARE NOW BEGINNING TO WAKE UP TO THE REALITY OF AN UNCERTAIN FUTURE BECAUSE OF THEIR OWN APATHY...

The last message Charley read before walking away was a question from the board:

...WHEN DOES A MELTING POT NATION BECOME SO CONVOLUTED THAT ITS ORIGINAL IDEAS BECOME LOST IN TRANSLATION ?...

"Nobody says stuff like that," said Charley, "at least not out loud.

"Alien-Nation indeed!"

Po' Boys

by Jim Elgas

Part I - Twenty-one-year-old Isaac Jennings lived in a small dying West Texas town. Jobs were scarce now that the manufacturing plant had closed down. Labor was cheaper south of the border. The plant execs had signed on to NAFTA (North American Free Trade Agreement) and 200 jobs vanished forever, including Isaac's. Needless to say this created a fair share of anxiety among the locals, especially those with families and mortgages. There seemed to be little opportunity for any semblance of what one might call a promising future.

Isaac weighed his only options. He could enlist in the service or sign on to welfare. Having been raised by a military father, he thought, "Why not, there ain't nothing happening around here." Maybe he could pick up a new trade and have a chance for college at some later date. He talked it over with his wife and they both agreed that it was a far cry from the conditions of welfare. If nothing else, Isaac had his own character to maintain and that inbred American determination to fend for himself.

They say that timing is everything. Shortly after his enlistment in the Guard, the catastrophic event known as 9-11 occurred. The national interest quickly took precedence as to where our troops would be deployed and where the conflict would be waged. Six years later and with limited downtime, Isaac, along with his band of brothers, found themselves still patrolling the streets of Baghdad with an uncertain game plan and a vague time-table for their return. Meanwhile, back on the home front, Isaac's wife faced her own battles with the finance company and creditors who were likewise looking out for their own interests.

Part II - Twenty-year-old Ishmael Akmad grew up in a family of 12 in the most economically depressed sector of Baghdad. He had lived his whole life under a brutal tyrant of a minority-led dictatorship. There were no aspirations of climbing the ladder to middle-class, because it never existed.

Ishmael's parents were devout Muslims who did their best at instructing their children on the sacred teachings of the Qur'an and the long history of their people. The only joys he treasured were found in the flesh and blood of his own family.

At the beginning of the war, Ishmael, along with many of his countrymen, had praised the ousting of the oppressive regime, which had subjugated them to the limits of human endurance. But with the ensuing descent into civil war and the subsequent loss of family members, including his mother and father, Ishmael's mind-set drifted over to the more radical factions of his religion in a desperate attempt at providing his own security. Sadly, joining the insurgents seemed like the only chance for survival.

It's difficult for any Westerner to comprehend such a scenario without having experienced these same circumstances and conditions in their own country, and impossible to state, with any certainty, what one might do if he were standing in Ishmael's sandals.

Part III - It was the first day of Ramadan, the holiest month on the Islamic calendar. The tribal factions and religious divisions came from far and wide to gather at the holy mosques in Baghdad. Tension was high and security units tighter than rusted lug nuts.

American troops filtered through the crowds in small platoons hoping to maintain the peace and solemn significance of the Islamic observance. Among them walked Isaac Jennings in full gear and keenly alert for any abnormal behavior. There had been reports earlier of insurgents planning to create chaos and alienate the Iraqi people from the troops, further fostering the growing hostility toward their occupation.

Isaac's concentration would occasionally lapse when feelings for his wife and daughter would randomly enter his thoughts. His third tour was up in two weeks and he prayed that he could just get through this in one piece. Though his prospects back home hadn't changed, he would now readily accept the offer of being unemployed as long as he was surrounded by his loved ones.

Part IV – Indiscernible, Ishmael strode calmly amidst the thousands of worshipers. Noticeable only to the trained eye were impressions of concealment beneath his clothing. That morning he had met with his cohorts and explosives were duct taped to his chest and torso. Afterward, they gathered in prayer for the success of his mission and drove him to the outskirts of the mosque.

Etched on his young face was the determination of a warrior, but deep in his heart came the warm memories of his family and the simple happiness they had shared. Even in their lifelong condition of dispirited poverty, they had somehow managed to stay together. He reflected, "I would do anything to return to that life," as tears flowed from what remained of his innocence.

From atop the Mosque, the Imam summoned the people to prayer. It was then that Isaac, with his finger on the trigger of his M-16 rifle, and Ishmael clutching the trip wire for the deadly explosives, caught sight of one another. For an instant they recognized themselves in each others' eyes—past and present. The prayers of the faithful rose up and surrounded their souls.

The moment of truth was upon them…

Author's note:

For further reference look up the story of Isaac and Ishmael in the Old Testament. They were the sons of Abraham, who had been promised a son to carry on the Hebrew race. Ishmael's mother was a woman of Arabic descent and Isaac's mother was Jewish… and the rest, as they say, is history. The descendents of these half brothers have been fighting and killing each other over their inheritance of land ever since. Just a couple of "Po' Boys."

Like Oil and Water

by Jim Elgas

~Assimilated Press Reporter~

Dateline: August 10th, 2050

The day and year had finally arrived. Four generations had come and grown, all of them witnesses to the often novel and sometime dead-serious attempts of Boingo Petrol to stem the endless flow of crude from their now defunct offshore hole at the bottom of the Gulf sea floor.

Long ago, the media had run out of land masses to compare the ever expanding size of their destructive slick. In its infancy, the area was compared to the dimensions of the principality of Andorra in northern Spain, which shortly thereafter expanded to the breadth of the Vatican, followed by the state of Rhode Island. Then they combined the states of Maryland and Virginia, and finally, whole regions like the upper Mid-West. News sources subsequently abandoned the practice when it encompassed two-thirds of the entire coastline of the United States. Eventually the blood colored current tinged the entire hue of the seven seas, decimating all marine life in its wake, and spontaneously created previously unimagined new industries in the economy.

Real estate developers, grasping for opportunities, bought up most of the shorelines for pennies on the Euro and successfully opened up novel franchise chains of kiddie tar sculpting establishments called "It's A Tar World After All". They attained instant popularity since the ancient art of sand castling had now become a distant memory handed down only as folk lore in a new line of fairy tale books. Sure enough, tar sculptures soon began lining the shores from Louisiana all the way to the White Cliffs of Dover, which over the years, had been renamed the Ebony Crags of Hell.

Scientists from NASA had ceased using infra-red camera shots in favor of color photography which offered higher resolution pictures and a truer rendition of the devastation. Meanwhile, an independent website had condensed forty years of satellite observation footage of the oil spill, set it in hyper speed, and posted it for the curious. It was said to resemble the visual effects of the lava lamps once popular with tripped out hippies in the 1960s.

Other irreversible earthly changes noted since the spill began were recorded in space photography from shuttle crews. The pictures show, depending on how you look at them, that the rounded curvature of our once perfectly symmetrical planet now oddly resembles a partially beaten piñata from a children's birthday party or that of a somewhat deflated balloon.

Boingo Petrol, or BP, has since tried to re-invent the company by changing its name several times, but not its initials, in an attempt to disassociate itself from the calamity they created. They went from Beyond Penalty, which caused quite a stir, to Blameless Pinheads, more aptly suited, and finally settled on Bygone Period. And although they failed miserably at every endeavor to stop the flow, they now had the chutzpah to claim success even though it was scientifically verified that the well had simply run dry on its own accord.

Immediately after the news of the oil spill cessation, the company began pouring billions of dollars into a revised media campaign for new offshore drilling platforms with the same time worn slogan of, "Drill Baby Drill." Thankfully enough, they were drowned out by an instant world chorus of dissenters shouting, "Never Again."

In a related story, Tony Hayward, the lead spokesman of BP, who brazenly stated at the outset of the disaster, "I just want to return to my life," was exiled, along with his family, by an angry majority of retired BP stockholders. He and his family now reside in the outer marshes of the Louisiana bayou and sources say they have been frequently and viciously attacked by a small remnant of genetically altered alligators and other denizens, who managed to survive the all but extinct habitat.

Rear View Mirror

(Objects May Seem Closer Than They Appear)

by Jim Elgas

When I was younger, my father would subtly pass out his pearls of wisdom without any hints of preaching. At the time, I did not seem to pay attention or ever imagine I would remember any of them, but somehow they continue to resurface during Zen moments in my life.

He was a child of the Great Depression and an eyewitness to firsthand misery. He believed that things were never as bad as they appeared to be and could always get worse.

So now, with the media labeled Great Recession upon us, one of his jewels has found its way back to the surface. I will relay its contents and a little story of how it was resurrected.

He used to say, "Once there was a man who was sad because he had no shoes, until he saw another man who had no feet, whose father was born with no legs."

It was a simple gilded statement laced in dark humor. It had remained dormant in me for many years, along with the wisdom it carried, until a recent trip to one of the discount grocery stores now prevalent throughout the country. It is not my intention to demean the store or anyone who shops there. It's all about living within your means, something that's been lost during the manufactured flush times of a few years back.

I recently shopped at one of these stores and noticed that everything was stripped down to the basics. There were three aisles and your choices were perishables, non-perishables, frozen food, and humbled vegetables. I immediately noticed the demeanor of the shoppers and the cashier manning the register. The mood was slightly somber with little conversation except for the back and forth between a mother and her child. Their spirits felt somewhat diminished but not yet desperate. I was reminded that the world is what it is and seldom how we would like it to be.

I paid for my items and carried them, bag-less, to the car. Once inside I noticed a poor soul on a bicycle riding down the produce ramp at the back of the store. He got off in front of a dumpster, pulled his shirt collar up over his nose and climbed in. Everyone who walked by ignored him or were oblivious to his presence. Minutes later, he emerged with a small plastic bag filled with his findings.

My heart sunk in my chest as he rode by and waved at me with a smile. As I watched him go around the car and disappear from the parking lot in my rear view mirror, I was immediately jolted by the sight of the largest American flag I've ever seen, flapping wildly over a recently closed car dealership...

"Happiness comes to those who appreciate what they have and are able to share their blessings with others."
-Cheechaboo

The GPS from Purgatory

by Jim Elgas

A lifetime of prejudice was all that 70-year-old Stan Quimby had been accustomed to. Growing up along the Illinois-Kentucky border narrowed his viewpoint considerably. He was the only one in his family who had remained behind. He spent his whole life, except for military duty in Vietnam, surrounded by people like himself whose definition of an outsider was anyone who wasn't born there. The rest of his siblings had moved north decades before, for better opportunities and to escape the hellish bigotry of the region.

His extended clan was planning a family reunion near Chicago. Stan's youngest brother, Mel, had the duty of sending invitations. He and his wife labored over the idea of extending a request to his older brother because of his rural bias. After much debate, it was decided to mail a lukewarm invitation accompanied by an outdated GPS device programmed to guide Stan to the event.

Mel confidently told his wife, "He won't come anyway, and if he does, the GPS will ensure he gets frustrated and goes home before he drives 20 miles."

On a hot summer day, Stan left Alexander County in his '57 Ford pickup pointed toward Route 51 and the City of Big Shoulders. He knew little about the GPS device, but managed to plug it into the cigarette lighter, and was taken aback to hear a woman's voice drone out an order to turn right onto the expressway.

"Well if that don't beat all," he drawled, "this'll be a cake-walk."

His expectations were soon thwarted by the blowout of a front tire. So he pulled off the road, and there he sat, surrounded by farmland with no cars in sight.

"Recalculating," groaned his strange GPS companion.

"What in Hades is that suppose to mean?" Stan grumbled. Climbing out of the cab, he scanned the horizon and spotted an approaching dot in the heat rising off the road. As it came into view, he began waving his arms for help. The car slowed, flashed its emergency lights and crawled to a halt. Out stepped a sun-silhouetted figure bowing his head as he neared. What sounded like, "hollow", emanated from the form.

"Well, hello to you, too!" Stan answered to the small man before him. "I got a problem here with my tire," he added, pointing to it.

The man smiled, bowed again, and motioned toward his car. Stan obliged and got in. Conversation was useless because neither of them understood the other. Ten miles up the road, they came to a gas station where Stan got out, bowed his head and thanked the stranger.

"Definitely Asian... Vietnamese maybe," he surmised, "but a real human being for sure," he mumbled to himself.

Back on the road and two-thirds of the way to his destination, Stan got hungry.

"Next oasis 3.2 miles," crowed the monotone voice from the netherworld of the GPS.

"That thing's a mind-reader, too," he said to himself in a mocking voice.

He had never been to an oasis before and was struck by the diversity of the people inside. He thought he had entered a foreign country. Hardly anyone spoke English and nobody seemed phased that they didn't.

"Where in the bejeezuz am I?" he asked himself.

Following the crowd to the buffet table, he grabbed a plate and began filling it. When he got to the register, the attendant totaled his bill and handed him a receipt. Stan reached for his wallet, but it wasn't there. He must have left it at the filling station and tried explaining his dilemma, but got nowhere. The cashier's only reply was, "No money, no eat."

Just then, the elderly woman behind him came to his rescue and promptly paid the bill. She was adorned in long flowing garments that entirely covered her head and body, except for a small opening for her eyes... eyes which conveyed a gentle smile. She was gone before Stan could make a choice of declining her courtesy or thanking her. After the meal, he climbed in his truck, humbled by the kindness of the woman. "Hmm...someone's trying to tell me something," he thought.

It was sundown as he approached Chicago. The GPS, recalculating again, began giving multiple direction options as he entered a construction zone. The speed limit had dropped to 45 mph, but most cars were still doing 70 mph while ducking in and out of traffic. He became disorientated and pulled off at the next exit, ignoring the GPS. The one-way street he entered led him west toward the United Center, an area he knew at once he didn't belong in. When he tried to turn around at a stop light, four shadowy figures quickly surrounded him. They broke his window and pulled him out onto the street. Before they could beat him, a huge African-American man, wearing a Guardian Angel beret, jumped in between them. The intimidated gang immediately took off. Quickly, the man turned to Stan and commanded, "Get!"

Trembling, Stan jumped in his truck, floored it, and never let up until he fish-tailed onto the expressway.

"It can't be much farther," he said, prayer-like, while silently promising to mend his racist ways if he ever made it back from this trip.

The GPS spoke up again, "Turn right at the next exit and continue one mile to your destination."

Looking up, he caught site of a billboard that read, "Welcome to Redemption Village".

He finally arrived at the reunion, worn and weary, but now buoyancy filled his soul...

He had been recalculated.

WILLIAM D. HICKS

Bill's Acknowledgements:

I'm an Illinois writer who lives by myself (any offers?). Contrary to popular belief, I'm not related to the famous comedian Bill Hicks (though I'm just as funny in my own right). Someday I'll publish my memoirs, though they'll most likely be about the famous comedian Bill Hicks' life.

In 2005 I received my Master of Written Communication degree. A group of master's students and I self-published **Save the Last Stall for Me**, *a bathroom anthology. Our pet anthology,* **Heavy Petting**, *is currently in negotiations with a publisher. A short psychological horror story,* **Twist**, *was released as an ebook in 2011. In addition, my poem,* **At Christmastime**, *will appear in the* **2011 Christmas Ideals** *magazine.*

My influences include David Sedaris and Stephen King. I want to leave my mark on one person. To make them smile. To make them laugh. To make them think.

My heartfelt thanks go out to Dr. C. Jeriel Howard who convinced me to get my master's degree. He also introduced me to Dr. Joyce Markle who taught me how to be funny in print. You rock Dr. Markle.

I also want to thank my deceased parents. Mom taught me that corpulent was a better word choice than fat. Dad gave me a reason to use that word. Plus, he inspired my love of reading.

WILLIAM D. HICKS

A Smoker's Journal

Parties, Patches and Pills

by William D. Hicks

On a snowy December day I attended a holiday party at a friend's house on the Southwest side. The house was cozy but to keep it warm all the windows remained shut. Around 30 guests, all having a good time, chatted about fashion, politics, hairstyles and exercise. They ate ham roll-ups and veggies and drank mixed beverages and beers. Many were smoking cigarettes. We were all having a great time. After several hours of socializing, smoke clung to my clothes. It masked the clean Dial Soap scent of my skin, the almandine conditioner in my hair and the Calvin aftershave on my face. But hey, what was a party without booze and smoke? Moreover, how could I complain, as I was one of the culprits. After seven years of tobacco-free living, I figured it was safe. It was a party after all. I'd had a few drinks. The smoke tasted good going down, filling my lungs. It made my alcohol-high even deeper. The world swirled, surreal. Infused with energy, my words felt fluid, my body energized, my thoughts acute. I was buzzed. Life was good.

That first puff was like eating a potato chip. I had one and I wanted another. I told myself I didn't *need* another cigarette.

I could practice abstinence. And I did. Until the next party. Then I had one, okay, maybe it was two cigarettes.

The secondhand smoke probably lured me in. It tied me up and seduced the smoker in me. The beers had been the secondhand smoke's accomplices. An alcohol downer was perfectly mated to a nicotine upper. They cancelled each other out I rationalized, so it was like having *nothing* at all.

I had become a star in the Cirque De Soleil of acceptable societal drugs. As I tight roped my way between alcohol and cigarettes, I felt like singing "flying high now" and "one toke over the line" and my own composition, "one cigarette between my lips and I've tossed away seven years of nicotine recovery."

I had fallen off the nonsmoking wagon. I inhaled. One puff led to many puffs. I admit it. I liked puffing. I was no longer a "recovering smoker." Now, I was on my way to being a pack-carrying member of a cult.

Worse yet, I was apparently addicted to more than one thing. After only two cigarettes, I became addicted to parties. Instead of asking the host, "Who will be there?" I asked, "How many people smoke? Filtered or non-? Menthol or regular? 100's or kings?" It took no more than a few months before I considered having my own "smoking parties." I even went out and bought 10 ash-trays to prepare.

Instead of hosting a bum-a-cigarette party I broke down and bought a pack. Benson & Hedges Light 100's in the box—my cancer stick of choice. Shortly afterwards, I started smoking at parties, smoking at home, smoking at work on breaks and before and after lunch; even smoking in my brand new Nissan. A sacrilege. This had to stop! After three months, I was smoking almost two packs a day.

A year after that second party and many cartons of cigarettes later, I realized smoking was a problem. I needed to quit. Originally, I quit cold turkey for one day after awakening with a bad sore throat. One day turned into seven years.

Now, however, for some reason, I couldn't do it. I couldn't

punt a pack of cigarettes through the goal post of recovery by myself. So I recruited medicine to be my quarterback at the kickoff. I would be the punter on the Nicotine Replacement Therapy team. I was going to try the nicotine patch.

My biggest problem was mornings. If I started smoking when I got up, I'd smoke all day. But my morning cigarettes were like my cup of coffee. They invigorated me. I *needed* them. Not so, the patch claimed. If I slept with a patch on— I'd win, beat the odds, and awaken craving-free. So one night I tried it. That night I had some incredible nightmares. I couldn't remember them exactly. When I awoke I felt the same as when I went to bed, tired. Like I'd just gone to bed. This happened night after night. I'd wear the patch, have nightmares, awake exhausted and haunted, my mind would be foggy all day. Every morning, in this state, I'd convince myself I needed something to help me wake up and I'd light a cigarette. This went on for weeks. Eventually, a friend who smoked explained that lucid nightmares were a normal side effect of the patch. So I quit—using the patch.

At this point, I decided I had to quit at any cost. I had heard that hypnosis might work. When I mentioned this to my oral hygienist, she told me about a hypnotherapist. My hygienist said that one of her patients, a night watchman, went and had quit for good. As he was a 20-year veteran smoker who lit up during his long boring night shifts, I figured hypnosis was worth looking into. I checked out the website and made an appointment. The cost was $200 for two sessions. At the first session, the woman therapist spoke very softly, in a hypnotic voice, about how smoking was just a habit like biting your nails. About how smoking was the cause of: cancer, the disastrous Exxon Valdez oil spill, and ugly babies being born to beautiful people. About how no one likes to kiss a dead ashtray. Well, she didn't actually say *those* things, but she did say how smoking was just a habit that could be broken. She also said that every time a person quit and started again they set themselves up for failure because this was conditioning their minds to think that smoking was okay. This was aversion therapy.

After this first session, I felt better and listened to her take-home hypnosis tape, included with her fee. The following day I had only three cigarettes before our second session. At this session, I nodded off. She wasn't boring, she had just hypnotized me by saying, "Close your eyes and relax. You are feeling sleepy. Your eyelids are getting heavy." I fell into such a deep sleep that I'm not sure what happened during this session. I kept going in and out of consciousness, hearing her voice, then nothing. All I know is that afterwards I didn't need a cigarette. Who knows what might have happened except for the fact that several hours later, I had a blowout fight with my best friend.

Voila! I was a smoker again. Even the take-home tape I got at my first session didn't help.

Nothing was working. I was growing tired of popping antihistamines to clear my sinuses before bedtime to prevent being awakened by coughing fits. My lungs needed a vacation. I needed a cure. I was against trying Zyban, a derivative of Wellbutrin, an anti-depressant drug. The cost equaled my first mortgage. For some reason, insurance wouldn't cover it. But I didn't want it to grow luxurious hair, or some other vain pursuit, I wanted it to get healthy. I knew two people, Mr. Jones and Mrs. Jones who lied to their doctors and said they were depressed so their insurance company would pay for the Wellbutrin. Who could blame them? You'd think insurance underwriters would *want* me to quit smoking, reducing my potential claims for emphysema, cancer and a Harvard education for my doctor's kids. But no. They would rather pay to turn me into a mechanical-lunged man after 25 years of smoking.

My brother Bob tried Zyban and said it diminished his cravings, but didn't stop them. When he first started it, his doctor recommended that over a period of weeks Bob reduce the number of cigarettes at the same time Zyban reduced his cravings. Spending $50 a week on medicine and another $50 a week on cigarettes felt exorbitant. Who was getting rich? Had some company secretly harvested Zyban and Wellbutrin from outer space? These drugs sounded alien. And, I refused to give this alien drug company any money that didn't pay for my nicotine fix. So I didn't try Wellbutrin or Zyban. I wouldn't support a Roswell-like, corporate game of greed. Bob, however, never held such high principles. Instead, he flailed with the pills and with smoking for months. He spent hundreds. He smoked, then took a pill. Took a pill, then smoked. Eventually, the cost became too much for him and he stopped taking Zyban and started smoking full-time. The Jones' stopped taking the Wellbutrin and started smoking as well. Later, however, Mrs. Jones suffered a heart attack. At 35 her fear-of-death and will-to-live instincts caused her to quit smoking cold turkey. This did not deter her husband, Mr. Jones, who still remains a smoker to this day.

After Mrs. Jones' heart attack, I desperately wanted to quit. A co-worker mentioned that her chiropractor also performed acupuncture "stop-smoking" sessions. Over the last four years I'd had patches applied to my arms and evil seeped into my dreams, what the heck, why not needles inserted into my body? While his website said nothing about acupuncture to quit smoking, my co-worker assured me that he performed this procedure. She said the cost was $75 for him to place needles in my wrist and apply acupressure to my ears. From what I've observed, acupuncture didn't end her smoking, but it reduced it greatly. Yet, for long-term stop-smoking results over a year, the CDC claims acupuncture is only about 27% effective. Still, 27% is better than zero. That's how effective the others have been for me—zero. I have an appointment to see this chiropractor in December.

Maybe next year when I attend my friend's Christmas party I will be smoke-free. But if not, I'm sure that someday a combination of patches, gums, inhalers, sprays, pills, needles and fear-of-death/will-to-live strategies will allow me to quit again. This time for good.

Energy Services

by William D. Hicks

"Energy Services, my name is Mary, how may I help you?"

"Hi...I..uh...oh it hurts so much."

"Ma'am what's wrong? Did you hurt yourself?" Mary asked, concern in her even voice. She twirled the phone cord around her forefinger. Usually she got people calling who had a wire short that required a technician to go out. But every once in a while...

"I think I dialed the wrong number. My chest feels like a ton of bricks... Ouchhhh," the woman's voice was fading, distant, pain ridden.

"Ma'am are you okay?" Mary stopped her twirling. This woman sounded ill. This wasn't her other typical call asking how they kept their rates lower than any other energy services, this was serious.

"No..I...I..it hurts...so...uh...dialed 911."

"No you dialed 811, this is Energy Services." This was the call. Every so often she got one of these calls. It made her nervous. But there was protocol for it.

In the 1900's there wouldn't have been, but things had changed drastically in the three hundred years since those primitive times. "Please turn on your Digital Photophone," Mary told the woman.

"Okay," the phone fell from the woman's hand, and

made a clunking sound as it hit the counter top in her kitchen. Shuffling noises followed as the woman made her way to where her television sat, the place people hooked up their Photophones. A slight click in the background alerted Mary to the phone being activated. She waited, then switched her line to the Photophone.

When the picture came in she could see the woman. She looked about fifty, and her color was bad. Pixelization technology had allowed for perfect skin tones on televisions. The screen showed that the woman was getting a trickle of blood to her heart, probably less to her brain. All these things ran across Mary's screen as the Photophone did a complete physical on the woman, whose name was Denise Brown.

Mary hit the mute switch. "I've got another one!" she screamed to the empty room. A man, standing five foot eight, with a balding cap, ran to her station.

"God," he said, "When we picked that 811 number, we hoped...we never expected to get this many people calling in." Then he punched in a code, which sent a message to the main computer.

Mary pushed the button which disengaged the mute signal. "Denise," she said. "Please place your hand to the television set, where you see me and Mr. Ramos."

The woman, almost crawling now, was white as an aspirin bottle cotton ball. "Will...it...will it help me?"

Mary looked at Mr. Ramos. They both smiled. Denise was fading fast now, her vitals were spiking. "Do it now!" Mary yelled.

The woman crawled faster and touched the screen in front of her. Mary saw her hand melt, almost through the screen, as if it were coming through the phone and photo wires and reaching into the room. Almost, but not quite.

Then a burst of exceedingly bright light exploded from the television and Denise flew to the ground, dead.

Mr. Ramos read his dials. "She gave us more energy than

some nuclear plants we have on line. What a boon that 811 number has been."

Just as the phone rang again Mr. Ramos arrived back at his outer office.

"Energy Services," Mary answered the phone, "My name is..."

"Isn't this 911?" the caller asked.

"No, but maybe I can help you."

Wisdom

by William D. Hicks

"The older you get the more you have to give up." My Dad told me this when I was a twenty-something kid. I didn't take it to heart then but as I get closer to fifty, I see the wisdom in his words. Over the last ten years, I've learned that this wasn't just Dad advising me what to expect as I aged. Instead, it was an omen because he was right.

In my forties, I had to give up alcohol, because I was an alcoholic. Well, that's not true. But I did give it up because it wasn't conducive to the medicines I took to relieve GERD symptoms.

What is GERD? Gastroesophageal Reflux Disease is a stress-related "me disease" that pretty much gives you acid indigestion every minute of every day, making your days miserable, and your nights worse.

To combat the GERD and my meds, along with the alcohol, I had to give up caffeine and orange juice. The only things I can now consume are bread and water. Oops...I lied. My doctor said bread and rice "expand in the throat" making my hiatal hernia act up which prevents me from swallowing and breathing. I could deal with the not swallowing, because then I'd have all the fun of eating plus all the joy of tasting it twice but the breathing part I can't compromise on. On top of all this, I had to give up jalapeño peppers and anything resembling spicy food... meaning anything with flavor. Now everything tastes like plain white bread, before it was a choking hazard.

More recently I found out I have diverticulitis. Oh, it's a fancy word meaning that anything made from seeds get stuck in little pockets in your colon. Pockets in my colon? I didn't even know I had trousers there.

So, now I must give up seeds? They're in everything. Seeds have graced every bun I've ever eaten. And what about seeds in fruits like raspberries, strawberries and bananas? Who am I kidding; almost all good tasting breads and fruits have seeds. Must I stop eating anything that tastes good? No, I was informed, soft seeds are okay. But they're soft after I chew them. Sorry, not good enough.

Are there any other things I will be required to surrender as I age?

My house? Will I become allergic to the mold that's lived and bred its offspring here for decades?

My car? Will I suddenly become claustrophobic and unable to ride in anything smaller than a tour bus?

My work? If I sneeze each time I touch a piece of paper can I get worker's comp or will my employers claim I have a "blue-flu-can't-do-any-work" type of ailment?

Perhaps I should just give up trying to figure this out. What I did come to realize though is that I needed to be Dad's age to understand his sage words. After all, who wants to take advice from a middle-aged man?

Just to be clear, I am middle-aged, so please don't think of this as advice. Take it as a sign or a warning if you will, for things that might come to pass...if they haven't already.

What Would You Say?

by William D. Hicks

If I told you what I was thinking
right at this moment, I'd
tell you...

That you should take that
broomstick out of your
ass because it's so far
up it's impaled
your heart

That you look like a
scarecrow with half
its smile rubbed away
by a lizard tongue
that darts out
between
its lips

That I want to wrap my hands
around your mole ridden,
mottled neck and choke
you until you breathe

your last
breath

That I dream about
you naked
in my
bed

That you disgust
me more than
steaming
dog shit

That I don't like to be
"yelled" at by an idiot,
even if it's only in *your*
head—so close your
squinty eyes and
shut the fuck up!

That I want to spit
in your face
every time I
hear your
voice

That you should
WORSHIP ME!

Why I Hate to Move

by William D. Hicks

Moving day was approaching. I hated all the necessary steps. Especially the phone calls. I often spent more time listening to Karen Carpenter musak than speaking with live people. At least I'd dealt with the following:

The Movers:
I'd gotten info via the Internet. Sounded good and it was fast. Still, who exactly had all my info? No doubt someone I didn't want to have it. Online, I usually faked it: The name's Billy D. at 0000 Some Street in A Town, IL 60000. But for a moving quote I had to use real information. I requested prices from a mover and the next day I had voicemails from 25. I even received flyers from across the continental U.S. and Hawaii. Two days later one innovative mover put all my stuff on his truck and held it hostage until I signed his 10 cents/pound declared value waiver. Later, I got the police involved to recover my belongings (mostly broken). "I'm having a garage sale," I told Officer Unfriendly.

The Police Department:
I thought Officer U could remember my garage sale in two days. Instead, he insisted I call the day before. Why? I thought it was so he could assign or hire enough officers to direct the

onslaught of drive-by traffic my "treasures" would surely generate. Boy was I wrong. Officer U mandated the call to hassle me about getting a permit, even though I read online that it was *not* required. He went on to explain that police protection was "a privilege, not a right." For the privilege of not receiving a ticket I had to give Officer U first refusal rights on my non-broken items, which he "negotiated" down to "free." In the end, I made enough to break even.

VOIPhone (Voice Over Internet Protocol phone service):

After engaging the tech via five emails and two calls, I figured she understood my timetable. I didn't currently have cable Internet or DSL, but my new condo would, so I needed VOIPhone installed in a week, after I moved. The following day I received an email that I would be switched the next day. "No," I emailed back. "Then I will be disconnected from the world." Without a cell phone (which I sacrificed to avoid brain cancer) my landline service wouldn't work with VOIP. I envisioned my personal business conducted via out-of-the-way conference rooms where I tied notes to snails and carrier pigeons. What were they carriers of, exactly? VOIPhone would read my email, stop the carnage and not make the switch. Wouldn't they? They had the power.

The next morning I awoke to a dead connection. I called to correct it and was informed a switch back would take 2-3 weeks. "But it only took you two days to *wrongly* disconnect me." I pleaded. If they could fit encyclopedias on a microchip couldn't they schedule a phone transfer date? No, the supervisor explained, VOIPhone's email center didn't communicate with their phone center in India. He credited me with a free month worth of service (three weeks of which I could actually use, after I moved). Without a phone or email, I felt so totally 1980s. I couldn't dial 911. Or the other 900 number I used as a lifeline. Could I live without these services? Could they live without my $2.99/minute?

With these phone calls out of the way, I only had a few more people to contact before I moved. I arrived at work early to accomplish my task. On my list was the closing lawyer, the mortgage broker, the developer and the cable TV provider. Also the Cancer Federation, to pick up what didn't sell at the garage sale. They supposedly wouldn't take "soiled" donations. Then the Salvation Army, who might take the stuff the Cancer Federation left behind. I'd call the upholsterer to pick up a chair I didn't want the movers to move and the bank to find out about a check for closing. I grabbed sticky notes and a pen as I headed off to the conference room. The snails and pigeons awaited my arrival.

Nine Asterisks
to the Perfect Condo

by William D. Hicks

I finally made it. I moved into a 3rd floor condo in the sky. It's perfect except...

The ceiling in the master bath began to lift when I put in a tension pole for the soap dish. Now, I'm installing a skylight under my neighbor's bathroom tub.

The living room is too small to fit the four foot couch I bought. It's a sectional, so one piece is in the living room, another is in the 2nd bedroom and the third fits nicely in the tub. Problem solved. Plus, it's a good lounging area to view my neighbor's tub above.

All the rooms have doors. Since the doors don't have any doorstops, knobs punch into the walls. Soon, all my walls will be as holey as a church confessional.

The elevator is slooooow. I can deal with slow, but not with the missing ceiling and wall panels. It's not a lift! Fix it!

My "secure" building has no doorbells so the lobby entrance is left wide open and even someone without an I.Q. can wander up to my front door. A homeless man once meandered in off the street to get in from the cold and asked for a place to sleep—I gave him directions to the developer's eight-bedroom house in Glenview.

The unit had a brand new washer/dryer. When the

washer is in spin cycle, it sounds like a plane taking off. This fits, because when the dryer is spinning it sounds like a plane landing (on gravel). The first time this happened, I expected a bomb siren and I did a duck & cover maneuver. To avoid this, I closed the laundry room door. It got so hot in there that when I opened the door I grew feverish. In my confusion, I took off all my clothes, sat down, threw some water on the dryer and reveled at my new indoor sauna.

The master bedroom has new air conditioning! But the developer was too cheap to install the right kind. The readout (on/off/AC/fan) faces the ceiling. Wouldn't be a problem—except the AC is mounted in the wall two feet from the ceiling. Sounds like a good reason (besides the obvious) to install ceiling mirrors.

Not only does the master bedroom have AC but so do two other rooms. It's not central air. So, every time I turn the air conditioners on for more than a few hours, I have to take out a home equity loan to pay the electric company. It got so bad I started to save for an AC Day, but in August every day was an AC day and I maxed out all my credit cards keeping my cool. Now I sleep on my balcony. I have a starlight view before I snuggle up in my sleeping bag, plus I get to go green when I fertilize the lawn every morning.

In my living room and both bedrooms, there are no ceiling lights. For light, I turn on the TV in the living room, the computer monitor in my second bedroom (my office) and the AC in the master bedroom so the red LEDs light up the ceiling. Then I feel my way around the room like Helen Keller. A second good reason to install mirrors. It would double the light in this room.

Design is in the Details

by William D. Hicks

You'd think that furnishing my condo with stylish furniture from Value City, Decorate Your Dive and Gnomes & Knick Knacks would satisfy my design sensibility. But any designer worth his naugahyde will tell you "design is in the details."

To that end, I spent hours on the throne reading home decorating magazines like *Black is Back*, *Architecture to Digest By* and *Couch Potato & Garden*. Next, I spent countless more hours—I've got the Preparation H to prove it—mulling over furniture store catalogs to determine accoutrements (French for expensive knick knacks made only in France). Every now and then, while holding decorating court, I'd throw a page at the bathroom wall to see if it stuck, literally or figuratively. I finally decided on a small piece of furniture to spruce my space.

Okay, so I'm not a handyman. But I thought I could put together a little cabinet with painted Grecian urns I found at Decorate Your Dive.

A carton arrived two weeks prior to the six-month anniversary of my order. The box could fit a Lear Jet. As I hoisted it into the elevator, I heard the rattle of moving pieces. The cabinet either needed assembly or it was shattered. Could particleboard and sawdust shatter? I checked to see if assembly information was indicated on the box; it wasn't. But the English was certainly absurd. It read "do no use knife, open." With no other options, I used my teeth. The packaging was heavy duty: In the end, I ended up with what I figured was 16 lbs. of bubble wrap to protect the screws, bolts and rubber end caps, enough cardboard to tile a high school basement plus a piece of Styrofoam® the size of Idaho used to prevent in-flight content shifting. This all cushioned a three pound faux-wood cabinet. In my mind, the $59.99 shipping and handling charges were justified.

Finally, I sorted the pieces into piles. In one pile, I had 300 screws (200 for a different cabinet), 22 bolts (a molecule-sized letter identified each) plus 50 end caps. Another pile had 13 jigsaw puzzle-shaped boards. The last pile had three hinges, although I only saw screw holes for two, and one pull for two doors.

I was all set to assemble until I realized I didn't understand the directions. English was only on the outside of the box. And Taiwanese was not something I learned in college.

So, I hired an interpreter. Mr. Chen Huang spent 24 days reading to me. Even though Huang did a great job of translating, oftentimes the meaning remained hidden. While he left a rich man, I still had questions. What was a toggle bolt? What were "cross" screws? Why did I need to use a rubber mallet to drive in end caps? It all sounded vaguely pornographic.

Since I didn't own any tools, I researched the ads in my decorating magazines. They sounded alluring and enticing: "Get the tools to satisfy your every need." I paid $49.99 to have them shipped overnight. When they arrived, my set included a screwdriver, a hammer and a knife. The latter might have come in handy when the box first arrived.

Despite my uncertainty and following too much goodbye-Saki with my Taiwanese friend, I assembled the cabinet. It looked great, even though it required two inches of Styrofoam to level it and the right hand door hung slightly askew.

Everyone who's seen it comments. My suspicion is it's the Grecian urns they adore.

I feel so accomplished having done it all myself, without even a basic understanding of the diagrams. While Huang could translate the words, he, too, couldn't comprehend the Tech-ese: Use diagram A, lift and separate toggle bolt C, then place it in hole B, securing it with an X bolt.

Yet, I find I still need a few more accoutrements. I have my eye on a silk pillow in the "Confucius Say: Decorate Today" catalog. It states: "worms do work, sit back and jerk" (I think they meant to say "sit back, you jerk," or "sit back, no work," but I'm not sure). This project sounds easier than the cabinet. All it requires are silkworms and a sewing machine. Once the worms spin their cocoons I will weave their silk into cloth and then sew the pieces together. Each silk worm costs just $3.99. For an additional $179.99 I can purchase the optional sewing machine. Worse case, I'll hire a Chinese seamstress to sew it by hand. God knows, I've been lonely since my Taiwanese friend went home.

Sunny with a Chance of Precipitation

by William D. Hicks

Sunny all day.
The weatherman called for snow.
25% right...75% wrong.
The viewing public loves him,
so the network TV website claims.
Where I work
instead of getting viewership
and a possible Emmy
he would get fired
or written up.
Oh how I long to be a weatherman.
I know—I know—
it takes years to
become a meteorologist
but not for me. I don't need any
training...because
I'll guess. I can't be
any more wrong.
50/50 I'll be 50/50 and
I'll still be doing better
than these

over-trained
over-confident
over-paid and often
over-weight
men who predict weather
like soothsayers reviewing
a magic eight ball.

Maybe—just maybe
I'll even make six figures
and get double digit bonuses
and have people throw themselves
at my feet with the gift of
sex for no other reason
than because I'm famous.
I'll get served a boatload of money
plus a side order of fame with my fortune.

I've figured out the secret to success.
Every day I'll predict the same weather pattern:
Sunny with a chance of precipitation.

Siblings

by William D. Hicks

"I told you so. I told you so," Nina said in a sing-songy voice, as she taunted her fifteen year old brother, Larry.

Larry tried to act like it didn't bother him. But it did, and he couldn't prevent the upset in his face from showing as much as he tried.

Nina was just thirteen years old and had braces. She smiled her "I win" smile. Larry couldn't help but notice how her teeth looked like shiny silver nuggets in the sun. He wished he were a miner and could remove them from her mouth.

"Mom, how come Nina gets to sleep over at Mary's house for the weekend, but you won't let me go camping with Tom and Peter?"

Nina looked like she wanted to know too. It was like a tennis match; the kids lobbed a question and the mother was expected to return it with an answer. Now the ball was in their mother's court, and they both looked at her in stark fascination.

"You two can be such brats to each other sometimes," Laura Kowslick told her children. "I don't know why you can't get along and not fight. One day you two will only have each other to rely upon. Then what? If you hate each other, you'll have no family."

Linda looked over at her children. They weren't absorbing anything she said. "You two will never learn. Larry, the reason Nina can stay over for the pajama party is that there will be adult supervision. Do you understand that? It's not because I am playing favorites here." She let out an audible sigh. How come kids thought that whenever a parent made a decision for their safety that it was either favoritism towards one, or meanness towards the other? She didn't know. "It's because there will be an adult who is responsible for her safety. That's why Nina can go and you can't, Larry."

"But Mom..." Larry moaned, looking like he felt slighted. "Peter is an adult."

"Peter Hendrickson is only eighteen years old. He is just barely an adult, and he certainly doesn't act like one."

Nina looked at Larry. Mother had returned the ball, maybe even aced it in a corner of the court. She doubted that Larry could touch that one. Her smile grew wide from the knowledge.

Larry stammered, "But..." in a whiny tone that was irritating.

Here was where Nina knew she had won and Larry had lost. This was Larry's begging tone, and one he seldom got his way with. It might have been because his voice sounded like a teakettle about to blow, or it might have been because he was a boy, but either way, Nina knew that her mother seldom gave in to Larry when he got this way.

"No buts," Linda said, then looked away having won the round. He couldn't go. She didn't trust that Peter kid. Larry might go along with anything Peter suggested. Linda shuddered at the thought, feeling the icy hands of fate run up and down her body. But she had to let go because eventually her son would make his own decisions with or without her approval. That thought did little to calm her jittery nerves.

"Peter, Peter, go away," she said. "Don't come back some other day," she continued unknowingly, under her breath.

The cold hands were back, making her shiver almost uncontrollably for one moment. "Please go away and leave my family alone," Linda prayed.

The storm came out of the east from Lake Michigan that night and whipped west across the Chicago area, taking with it tree limbs, paper and the pollen which had satiated the land all summer. Rain poured down like a weeping giant, his cries the thunder of the night, the lightning his angry tantrum.

Larry awoke several times that night. The final time, he was awakened by the ringing of the telephone. Someone was calling who wanted him to get out of bed. He ran down the hall, faster than Nina, and more alert than his mother and father. He got to the ringing device first, hearing the rhythm of his sleeping family around him.

"Hello?" he asked, in his sleep heavy voice, wondering why anyone would call so early on a Saturday. His watch read just 7 a.m.

"Let's party!" the other caller said enthusiastically.

"Who the hell...?" Larry started to ask who it was, then he recognized the gruff voice as his best friend's. Peter wanted him to come out and see all the damage the storm had done.

"Why so early?" Larry asked tiredly, wanting to return to his warm bed.

"Early bird catches the worm," Peter replied, full of energy. "Meet me at my house in five minutes."

"Never do it," Larry replied. Even though he wanted to go back to sleep, he said, "I've got to get dressed first. I'm not usually—"

"Ten minutes then. But hurry."

Click. The line went dead. Peter had hung up.

Larry dressed as fast as possible, rushing, but still trying to remain quiet. He didn't want his parents to know he was still friends with Peter. They would surely question him about his getting up so early, and Larry knew he was a bad liar.

Larry slid into his ripped Levi's and put on his black Metallica T-shirt. The one he had bought because Peter loved the heavy metal band so much. Finally he put on his shoes. The first shoe, a Reebok, slipped from his grasp and went flying through the air like a fat white bird. It hit his dresser with a thud. Larry couldn't help but think of all those Batman shows with "Thud", "Ugh" and "Bang" in them. The shoe, had it been in one of those episodes, would have been a wingless bird and would have read 'squawk' when it hit the dresser. A nervous laugh crept into Larry's throat and escaped. He feared what would happen if he got caught.

He crept down the stairs quietly. He listened to the sounds of the house. The seven-day clock ticked the time away in the living room below, and a dripping faucet seemed to drip in harmony. The old floor boards moaned beneath his weight, and he stopped, hoping no one had heard them.

If only his parents could understand that at fifteen he should be able to pick his own friends, then he wouldn't have to sneak out like this. But after Peter had gotten busted for pot possession, Larry's parents had forbade him to stay friends with the eighteen year old. Even though Peter only had pot for his own pleasure, Larry's parents wouldn't listen. They thought Peter was a drug dealer or something just as evil. Larry knew better.

Listening, he still heard his father's snoring, and the slow rhythmic sound of his mother's breathing. The only one he couldn't hear was Nina. She snored lightly when she slept, and talked in her sleep. He moved forward on the steps again, almost at the bottom.

"What are you doing?" a voice whisper-yelled down the stairs.

Larry almost jumped out of his skin, feeling like some ghoul had jumped out at him unexpectedly in a house of horrors. His heart tripled its beat, his testes hiked up like they wanted to hide, and he almost flung himself forward on the stair. Instead, he grabbed out for the railing and caught himself, then instinctively looked up the stairs. Nina stood there in her pink robe, tied loosely around her body. She was beginning to grow breasts, and the slight bumps under the robe showed where they were sheltered. Her hair was in disarray, as long strands fell around her face, and other pieces were matted together in snarled knots.

"None of your beeswax," Larry whisper-shouted back. His anger was almost visible as he clung to the safety of the hand railing.

Nina walked down the stairs now, not worrying about the noise they made.

Larry grimaced every time she hit a squeaky board. And there were lots in the hundred year old home where they lived.

"Shhhhh."

"Not until you tell me where you're going at this time of the morning."

Of course he had no choice. He either told her, or she would make trouble. But if he told her the truth, then she might just tell anyhow. "I'm going to meet Sarah for breakfast."

"Sarah, your girlfriend?" Nina didn't believe him, but she decided to play out the game.

"Who else?"

"Well, I happen to know that she went to visit her aunt in St. Louis, so unless you're planning on taking a bus or flying there, I doubt it."

"Uh...well...I missed her so much..."

"Don't lie to me Larry. You're still friends with Peter Hendrickson. Jenny Sarape told me she saw you two hanging out near the swings just last week. I didn't believe her until she described that putrid jeans jacket you wear with all those patches on it. Then I knew she was right." Nina's face was tight with an anxiety he had never seen in it before. She didn't look at all like the girl who had taunted him just six months before when she had gotten to go to a pajama party, and he had been unable to go camping with Peter. She looked more like his mother. Fear showed in her eyes now. "Tell me the truth. Are you going to his house?"

"Yes. But please don't tell Mom or Dad," Larry replied, incapable of coming up with a story. "Please," he begged her in his whiny tone.

It was the exact same tone he used with Mom, Nina knew. The one that never worked. Yet she couldn't snitch on him forever or he would snitch on her forever. "I won't tell. But you owe me one."

That was the sister he had grown to hate, the one who couldn't do a kind deed without repayment. "Fine."

"Be careful. Sarah said that Peter beat up Tony Vetrano, just because he accidentally bumped into him on the street. Tony's that kid who won't even catch butterflies because he doesn't want to hurt them. Peter's bad news. Everyone else knows that but you."

"No he's not," Larry said, then jumped down the remaining stairs and left the house. He wanted to slam the door, but was afraid to wake up his parents. How could Nina say such a thing? Maybe Tony had said or done something she didn't know about. That had to be it. She was only thirteen, he reminded himself, too young to understand the ways of men.

Papa's Poltergeist

by William D. Hicks

Father passed on some time back. Not that he passed on anything; he ate everything in sight. What a stupid term for dying.

When did Dad die? I remember it was cold and the frost had turned the windows pale white. I can only say he was gone before the iris bulbs broke free of their frozen hibernation.

It was 1984. I'd recently broken up from my lover Daniel. I'd moved to Denver and was feeling like an ex-patriot, hardly knowing anyone, and glued to my job like a fly to paper. The money was good, even if they treated me like an indentured servant. I made a perfunctory attempt to attend my father's funeral, but I was too busy with the Endine Acquisition. I sent flowers, but I didn't really care if I attended or not, it wasn't a priority. In the end no one but the minister attended. I sent the Catholic Church a bonus check to ease my guilt. After that I just couldn't bring myself to visit the cemetery. Not with his gravesite next to Mom's.

Dad killed himself. He devoured Domino's Pizza, dozens of Dunkin Donuts, and green beer after green beer, followed by that foul tasting, coffee-ground bitter Guinness, on his most hallowed holiday, St. Patrick's Day. Maybe overindulging filled the void my gayness created.

You know that it was really me who killed him. Me and my coming out. What a joke, that he might accept and still love me. He would have killed me with his own hands and gone straight to hell for the crime rather than live through the humiliation of his poker buddies finding out about my gayness, which they did.

Now in 1985, after attending a conference in Chicago, I was back in my hometown. And Dad visits me. Not like a Holy Trinity ghost, with omens of evil, or foreshadows of things to come. No, he comes to spite me and make life miserable. Remind me of my shortcomings. Remind me that I am not a man, at least not to him.

He visits me. Not in my mind. Not in my dreams. In the flesh. If you could call his ephemeral black and leathery seal skin flesh. It stretches over bones too brittle to be anything but toothpick-imaginings from my own mind. I guess I deserve it, after failing him in life.

When he comes, he explodes, something he was prone to doing in life. His gaseous self splits into hundreds of brown shards then reassembles. His yellow eyes bore deep holes into his gay son. "You must make peace," he says. Sallow skin, pulled taut across a once-freckled face, makes his searing eyes that much more grotesque. They are accusatory, like I am a piece of shit, the thing which caused him this painful death. His body was so frail, but his mind held all that hurt, the upset of a father destined never to have his name carried down through another generation. That from his manhood he produced not a man, but a thing which resembled a man in every way, except that which was most important to him.

Pills and Papa. Dad rises nightly from my kitchen faucet, like a reverse-genie, come to take three wishes away. I drink my water and take my sleeping pills, and laugh that he must know of my sleeplessness. Nightmares keep going like that ugly pink bunny.

I awake again at 3 a.m. Some horribleness I can't remember flashes through my mind. I move through the night like a ship on a black sea. Light will awaken me fully and I can't take that chance. I bump my shin into the hard-edged dresser and sit down at the hotel desk. Flipping on the nightlight, which looks like a space alien's mother ship, I scribble a note to Daniel.

"Daniel," I write, "I know your father died recently, do you want mine?"

What a shamefully disrespectful note to send someone on the death of his much-loved father. He'll just think I'm insane, hell, maybe I am, but what can he do about it in Denver? Nothing. Shit, I love Dan, I even liked his father. What might I write if I didn't care? I turn off the nightlight and toss out my scribbling.

At least Daniel's Mom is still alive. I miss mine.

Mom, she's been dead six years, two months, one week, two days. Hours? Minutes? Seconds? I know those too. The end came suddenly, as a blood vessel in her brain changed her innocently dumb stroke-face into that of an IRA bomb victim. As I sat smoothing her once shimmery red hair, now disheveled and gray, talking about her coming home with me after the hospital, her final moments came on like a short burst of gunfire that seemed to last an eternity. Her face peppered with shrapnel shock.

"I watch you, Dad, believing my gayness was Mother's fault, Mother who was strong and set limits and taught me how to mend my tattered britches and wash the laundry by separating colored from white underwear. I know you blamed her. You perverted our relationship, turned it into some fucking sick Freudian nightmare. Believe what you want, you asshole, but it wasn't true!

"You made me the product of a strong mother so you

never had to feel your seed had anything to do with who I became. But if you want the whole truth, listen up; mother was strong because you were weak, with food, booze and other women. Sorry to ruin your perception of me as a drag queen wearing Mom's high heels while she converted me into the little daughter she always wanted, but Daddy Dearest, here is the gruesome, blinding-headlight flash out-of-nowhere truth: a gay man was your best friend; a gay man cut your hair; a gay man was the middle-aged Air Force sergeant with stripes and power over you. Mother loved me, for who I was. Dad, you did not. My distance from you broke her heart; I killed her.

"Yeah, and I am killing her now. By having sex with any man who looks my way. By taking absurd risks. By bare-backing, not always using condoms, whoring around. Mother was waiting for me when the hammering strokes hit, believing they were stress headaches, things brought on by too many years of worry and concern, over me and you, Dad. I found her on the floor barely able to talk. All she said was "Be careful" and "I love you." I committed matricide, killing the one person who loved me with all my faults, because all I ever wanted was your love Dad, and any man who would put out I fell madly in love with, if even for just an evening.

"Dad, you must know that I held your dear friend Jack in my arms after the death of his wife, and then had sex with him, changing him forever, allowing him to see that two men could truly be intimate, that gayness was not a loss of manhood, but an affirmation of sameness. To have outed your then best friend, to have shown him the 'wild side', wasn't enough. No. Jack moved away, leaving hollowness in your heart that you could never voice or ease. Dad, I believe you know these things, now, and come back to torment me and make me suffer as you suffered the loss of your best friend."

A grimace envelopes Dad's face.

"You used to say I whined too much, that I was weak like

Mother, like a woman. 'Be a man,' you'd say. 'Take it like a man.' Yeah you modified this one when I came out didn't you, because you knew I took it like a man, every time another man told me to bend over, I took it only as a man could. Bastard."

"You disgust me." Dad finally says.

"Another line you made famous after I came out."

"I'm not disgusted because you are gay."

A new line, have you learned something in your afterlife psych-support sessions? "No," I say. "I disgust you because I loved men."

"You no more 'loved' those men than I was faithful."

A truism. You are learning.

"Once upon a time, I did love a man. Daniel. He quickly grew tired of my cheating, my lies, and left me. Guess where I learned how to do those things?"

"Excuses are like buses, everyone uses one to get somewhere. We all make excuses." Dad says, "To justify mistakes."

"I was your worst, I can see it in your dead eyes," I reply, "Daniel, he was not a mistake. How can you belittle my only significant relationship?"

"Perhaps not. Blaming me for your life is what you do best. Don't use me as an excuse any more. I'm dead. Get the car."

I get the car. He is my father after all. Even ghosts retain parental rights.

As I sit in the driver's seat, Dad hobbles over to the passenger side, lifting his almost useless leg into the car. I remember when he broke it. My fault. Not that I broke it. Dad said the path to mother's grave wasn't too icy, but I knew his cataracts were bad and the markers were shadowy ghosts beneath recent snow. When Dad fell, his leg snapped like a dried piece of tinder wood. He screamed as the bone protruded from the wound. Compound. Amazing Dad could ever walk again. Sheer stubbornness.

"Take me to your mother."

The drive to the graveyard is almost silent, except for the pinging punctuation of the jagged rain, which invades the silence I might otherwise enjoy.

The graveyard is unkempt, next door to a housing project sprawled out like a tumorous growth, Chicago's answer to Belfast's graffiti messages of social injustice. The walls full of dirty love-messages scrawled in luminescent green paint imprisoned by blood-red hearts. Define confusion: trying to figure out who-loved-whom-when by the hearts and dates painted on the wall.

Cabrini Green gazes at its potholed, drive-by-shooting streets where grass refuses to grow, down toward the once expensive but now poorly kept-up markers of the Rosehill Catholic Cemetery. It scares the Irish-American alderman who drive past tattered remains of clothing hung from lines strung across back porch rafters, past black kids dancing to rap words they call music, singing about how to escape by beating back white oppressors. I'm one of the Irish-Americans who drives past and stares, scared to enter this world, but oddly drawn to the markers of my once living parents. We Irish came to America to escape the oppression of being religiously different. Being different scares us, the poor scare us. We escaped a land infected by our own hate only to infect another. You can never escape your religion or your skin color or your own feelings of inadequacy.

The blacks viewed us through their own eyes; we were the enemy, not people who understood their struggle and plight. All they saw was all we saw: the color of our skin shades our outlooks just as surely as the label Irish makes people believe we're all drunks.

"Watch out!" Dad yells.

We almost hit a drunk swaggering across the road. I swerve, missing him barely. Dad curses my driving.

"You're dead Dad. Goddammit." I speed up as the rain pounds on the hood.

"You're not."

"I understand you don't want to share your eternal resting place with me, your piece of crap queer son. I might molest the angels," I swear out loud, spit flying from the corners of my mouth. What a mourning son I make, anger flying from my mouth like a petulant wild-eyed child instead of the red raccoon-eyed grieving orphan I am.

"You don't believe that shit!" Dad's face glows orange from my dashboard lights, unclear like an out-of-focus photo.

Now I'm doing 70 mph in a school zone, no one's awake; everyone's tucked in their beds safely dreaming about sugar plum faeries, not real life fairies. I'm hoping my car kisses the tail end of a parked truck on a blind curve and Dad goes up in a puff of smoke in the screeching scene. I'm sleep deprived. If I die now will this nightmare ever end?

"Get us to the cemetery in one piece."

"Why?" I ask, but take my foot off the gas instinctively.

"Just do it." Dad's last words on most topics closed to me, his fruit son, and his answer to all subjects we disagree upon.

When we arrive, Dad looks so old. His skin is wrinkled like a sun-dried pomegranate, his hair gray, and his yellow teeth show blank gaps between them. His face still looks bloated from cancer, even in its sunken state, from years of binge eating and exploring all the limits of addiction, pools of skin sag where his neck and chest meet. He opens the car door, almost falling face first. I reach for him. He's gone.

I tumble out. He reappears.

Dad takes one step, then straightens. I notice his fatness has returned, he is again full of blubber, like a pregnant whale. Stooping from his massive weight, his pink eyes make him resemble a hog. A dumb happiness permeates his face, then an explosion escapes him. His ephemeral self shatters.

When he comes back together, he straightens up. Now his hair is red-gray, his eyes have lost their filminess. He's the Dad I remember after I came out and he will be full of liquor. I imagine I can smell it. Drunk, fat and full of himself, the Dad I knew.

He takes another step. His hair turns bright red, deep as the day is dark. Black hip hugging pants grace a trim waistline. His limp is gone, his eyes are full of life and joy. His skin is taut, his body, trim and muscled. I don't remember him like this, full of vim and vigor, smiling. Did I ever see him like this? Yes, in old photos Mom kept, the one time I snuck a peek at them in her underwear drawer. In these photos, Dad and Mom had been married a short time and I was a tiny baby in her outstretched loving arms.

Dad moves a few more steps. Now he's a teenager, Dad with a thick red curly mop of hair instead of the old military cut of later years. His teeth are white and gleaming, none missing, none yellow. His face baby-soft, smoothed of life's legacy, no fat, no wrinkles, just youth and hope.

"I am dead. Really. Please let me go." Dad moves toward Mom's grave, her marker, an Angel overlooking his own. He stares at Mom's grave, and cries. He faces the headstone and speaks. "I did my best."

I move toward Dad's marker, a large Celtic cross. Odd that he chose that since he wasn't religious before he died. Mother would not have liked the blasphemy. But I expect Mom would forgive him his mistakes, as she forgave me mine, though she never materializes to grant him or me absolution.

"I did my best too," I say.

Dad dissolves into the earth of his grave as the sun breaks free of the black horizon.

I stand by my car. Tears stream from my eyes. I hate crying. I haven't cried in years. But what else can I do? Dad rose from his grave to prove that he was dead. I stand for a few more moments, looking over toward where my parents are buried. From where I am, I see a skunk scurrying by a few yards away, moving as if in a hurry to get somewhere, as if I am invisible.

By the roadside, an old beater roars up, "Hey man, don't let no ghosts out" several teens yell. They laugh. They speed away.

"I won't," I say to thin air. "Not anymore."

Granny Goes to the Nursing Home

by William D. Hicks

"Baby girl, you went before we left the house. When we get there you can go again."

"Yes Granny we're almost to your new home."

"Of course she knows it's a retirement home, honey. She picked it."

"No, baby girl it's not the place we took Grandpa. And no, it doesn't have a swimming pool."

"No baby girl, what you saw was a pond. Grandpa's in a graveyard."

"Yes, it would be nice. Though you'd probably drown if you were in a coffin in a swimming pool or a pond. It's not like a boat baby girl."

"No, I don't want you to drown, Granny."

"Honey, I was NOT being disrespectful."

"Baby girl, drowning is when someone can't breathe and dies."

"No, it's not like when you accidentally flushed your frog down the toilet."

"Okay, when you flushed Mr. Froggy down the toilet. I hate saying that name."

"I am telling her the truth, honey. Well, I guess it's sort

of like that, except that Mr. Froggy did not choose to go swimming in the toilet."

"Don't cry baby girl, it was an accident. We all know you just wanted him to be closer to the water."

"No Granny, I don't plan on having any accidents like that with you."

"Yes baby girl, after you die you go to a graveyard. No, there are no froggy graveyards."

"Granny, we do love you. I swear."

"Can you all be quiet so I can concentrate? Traffic is getting heavy and I don't want to have an accident."

"I'm NOT trying to scare anyone honey—it's just that I need some quiet time."

"No baby girl, Daddy's not mad at you. Please don't cry."

"Yes, Granny we are almost there. Only 30 more miles."

"Yes Daddy can have an accident too honey, so don't cry over the frog. I mean Mr. Froggy."

"I wasn't being mean honey. I just hate saying Mr. Froggy; an adult man shouldn't have to say that name."

"Oh baby girl, I'm not mad at you."

"No Granny it's not out in the boondocks where we will never see you again. We are NOT like those people who dump their unwanted pets on the side of the road, I swear. We will come visit."

"Honey, I'd rather not stop at the antique store right now. Maybe on the way home."

"Granny we're NOT trying to get rid of you so we can go shopping and redecorate your room. Remember, you picked this new care facility."

"Honey, I am NOT being surly. I was just explaining, I swear."

"Yes baby girl, if we stop at the antique store on the way home, you may get one scoop at the ice cream parlor inside."

"No you may not Granny. You know you have trouble with milk products so ice cream is out. But they probably have really good rice pudding for dinner. Please don't cry Granny."

"Oh baby girl, don't start crying too. I know you miss froggy. I mean Mr. Froggy."

"You're not? Then what's wrong baby girl?"

"No it's not like when Mr. Froggy died, we can visit Granny."

"No not at the graveyard, she won't be dead."

"You're NOT helping things Granny. We're not dumping you—we will come and visit! Can't you see she's upset."

"I'm NOT yelling, I'm trying to get Granny to listen, honey."

"Oh baby girl, please don't cry. We'll all miss Granny."

"Yes we will Granny. Please, don't you start to cry too. I'm sorry, I didn't mean to sound angry or yell. Please don't cry."

"Honey, I was NOT trying to be mean. I swear. Can you talk some sense into those two...oh no, not you too."

LARRY KING

Larry's Acknowledgments:

LK: Don't forget to update this placeholder text and load to the Finals File before the deadline!

This is the part of the book where I need to insert my acknowledgements. Until I have time to do it justice, here's a stream of consciousness to approximate the length of the piece.

On to the second paragraph of my heartfelt gratitude to the people who have supported me since I decided to start writing, two years ago. Let's assume the first paragraph thanks my dear bride Judy and our great sons Tim, Sean and Chris for staying out of my hair while I write. I love them and all that true crap. Maybe that's the last paragraph. We'll see. Of course, I must thank my First Draft Review Team: Heather, Amy, Mary and Marc. And the Panera Gang: Alisa, Colette and Renee. Plus the Closet Geek Book Club: Kim and Amy (again!). TY to the AHA team, then there's Mindy, Jeannette, and obviously Jim Elgas, that free-thinking, story-telling, pot-stirring, ever-inspiring force that blew into my life and gave me an opportunity to write for "The Almanac of Arlington Heights", that beloved "little yellow book" he and Mindy created. I haven't looked back since.

What else did they say to put here? Literary influences: Ray Bradbury, George Carlin and Dave Barry. How I write: Under the influence. Why I write: It's a kick and a challenge, and I can leave something of record which might put a smile on someone's face that I don't even know, and how cool and fulfilling is that?

Wrap it up with a shout out to the Arlington Heights Memorial Library even though I'm a Buffalo Grover. Did I mention I grew up with four brothers in Flint, Michigan and have lived in Chicago for thirty-something years? Of course thanks to Mom and Dad. That ought to do it.

LARRY KING

The Fluffy Stuff

by Larry King

It's said the Eskimos have over a hundred words for snow. I only have six, but they're all four-letter ones. Don't get me wrong. I love the four seasons we experience in the Midwest, but there are parts of Old Man Winter's repertoire that would try the patience of Job. Then again, Job lived in the desert and never had his beard frozen while snow-blowing the driveway.

An individual snowflake is a thing of beauty. When a few million of them decide to get together and hang out on your car while you're at work, and the nearest thing you have to a scraper is a CD case, it's no longer beautiful. On the streets, snow interferes with harmonious human interaction. I don't mind those drivers who have to adjust during the first few snowfalls. It's the ones who still haven't figured it out by March that make me want to ram them with a county snowplow.

When did our local news programs decide an incoming snowstorm is reason to push the panic button? You'd think we live in Florida the way they warn us and overreact. It's Illinois folks. It snows. It's not news. You don't need to tell me shoveling is strenuous and backbreaking. Regardless of which shovel design you use, curved blade or straight, curved handle or straight, after an hour moving wet heavy snow your spine feels more curved than straight.

But you have to give snow its due. It looks magnificent

when giant puffy flakes float and dance in the air before adding to the brilliant white carpet. Or when the wind carves the snow into drifts transforming a row of garbage cans into a miniature mountain range.

You know who looks at snow and sees real beauty and potential? Kids. There are so many ways they delight in it: sledding, making snow angels, just playing in it. No agenda, just enjoyment. A kid appreciates the different kinds of snow. Heavy and wet? Perfect for snowmen, snow forts, and rock-hard snow balls that explode like fireworks when thrown against a brick wall. Light and fluffy? Easy shoveling, and in a good wind just toss shovelfuls into the air to make your own personal snowstorm.

Then there are snow days! There's no better feeling than when school or work is unexpectedly cancelled. Sometimes when Old Man Winter is a wizard with a blizzard, we all prosper. But snow days are as rare as a rainbow in January. By Groundhog's Day it seems like winter will never end, whether the big rodent sees his shadow or not. A lot of folks just surrender to the season and become snowbirds. I can see the benefits of this: enjoy the holiday season with a month or so of snow, then blow. Leave the snowdrifts in the rearview mirror.

As in many things, one can look at the salt truck as being either half empty or half full. Use snow to your advantage with this cheap, easy, and unforgettable way to tell that someone special how you feel. Timing is critical, it must be right after a snowfall leaves a perfect blanket on your yard, driveway, or vacant lot next door. Put on your boots and get ready to create the best non-Valentine's Day valentine ever. At the bottom of your canvas, shuffle your feet and move ahead in the snow, leaving a path behind you. Here's the tricky part: shuffle a giant heart shape. Okay, here's the really tricky part. Jump into the heart and shuffle your statement of love: initials and plus sign. My snow art heart showed L+J, and Judy loved it, even took a picture. Now that's money in the bank. Don't be too ambitious; adding an arrow unnecessarily complicates things. Also, don't indulge in any 'adult antifreeze-type beverages' before attempting your heart, or it may end up look like a kidney with drunken cursive writing.

In a list of snow's pros and cons, the cons are adult-oriented irritants: extra chores, traffic complications, and cold-weather body-aches. The pros are joy-filled: playing in it, watching it fall, and in the spring watching it melt. An enterprising kid can turn cold snow into cold cash with a shovel, some hard work, and of course a sensible hat.

Maybe the secret to dealing with snow is to embrace it as a child and endure it as an adult. Much like life itself.

The Spummer Season

by Larry King

There's a stretch in the year when the seasons blend between Spring and Summer. I call it Spummer, that time from about April 15th until the 4th of July: Uncle Sam's payday until his birthday. It's a great part of the year with a lot happening and even though the days are longer, it seems the hours are shrinking. Before I know it, we're into the dog days of summer and I still have half my spring projects left. Yet it's important to slow down and enjoy the celebrations, fun, and opportunities the season brings, before it gets past us.

A couple of important Spummer occasions are Mother's and Father's Day. It's good that as a society we take two days a year to "Honor thy father and thy mother." I don't know if Hallmark has been selling cards since that commandment was handed down, but I wouldn't be surprised. Although let's be honest, Father's Day seems like a bit of an afterthought. Besides having to share billing at the card store as "Dads and Grads", it's rare to find an elementary school teacher with the foresight to plan a Father's Day art project before school is out.

Spummer has those wonderful few weeks when Mother Nature treats us to her yearly floral fireworks display. Explosions of white dogwood tree blossoms burst among the deep red maples which prepare to launch a million tan helicopters. Fading purple lilacs hang on as the grass gets ever greener, all beneath an umbrella of eye-jarring blue sky. Our street is lined on both sides with crabapple trees the city planted in the easements years ago. When they bloom, it becomes a tunnel of brilliant pink and I marvel at the foresight of the people who planned this lovely piece of natural artwork. Of course, in five months I'll curse the idiots who planted those pseudo-fruit dropping, mess-making trees.

Spummer is the beginning of my annual vegetable and flower crapshoot. Soon I'll find out if the peas are prosperous or piddling, and how this year's tulip display turned out. Will the bulbs I carefully planted last fall in well thought-out color combinations burst from the ground in beautiful bunches, providing a little touch of Holland here in Illinois? Unlikely. More likely, a few scrawny sticks will poke their red and yellow heads out before a light wind blows away their petals. Either result assumes some rotten squirrel didn't dig up the bulbs and haul them away the day I planted them.

The first tastes of "outdoor food" come in Spummer: that juicy snap of a grilled brat or sausage, the cool sweetness of the freshest strawberries of the year, and potato salads in a variety of white and yellow shades. Pop and beer is extra cold and refreshing, bobbing in tubs of half-melted ice, numbing the hand as a selection is made. Barbeques and picnics feel special, not worn-out like at the end of summer. By Labor Day I'm ready to turn vegetarian at the sight of another over-cooked burger or blackened, shriveled wienie.

Spummer also spawns the soundtrack for the rest of the year. We begin to hear the tunes that will provide the background music at beaches, bonfires, ball games, and weddings. Try to guess which of the hits coming out now will be the Songs of Summer. The ones that have the irresistible hook, the driving beat, and the annoying chorus that will soon emanate from every speaker on the planet for months on end.

The best thing about Spummer is how the world flourishes with people. There's no excuse for staying inside as the days get longer and warmer, so we take advantage. Baseball diamonds and soccer fields teem with kids in uniforms of every color, while adults cheer, chat, stretch, and soak it in. On a sun-splashed day the world is overrun with people doing everything from walking to biking to lounging on the deck with a good book. There's fresh air, and fresh hope in the air as we're determined that this is the year we'll paint that fence, lower that golf score, do whatever that thing is we've been waiting months to do. Only do it better this year.

Spummer is ripe with opportunity. It's a time of celebrations, hope, and growth but is over before we know it. We need to savor Spummer, because soon enough it will be Sautumn.

Road Games

by Larry King

On summer road trips when I was a kid, the best chance
to gain points in the license plate game was when Dad would
pull into a national or other semi-documented major tourist
attraction.

"Montana!" One of us kids would shout.

"All right! That makes 32 state's plates we've seen."
My oldest brother tallied.

"Florida. Nope, already got it."

We'd drive through long rows of massive parking lots,
our eyes scanning at bumper level.

"Indiana. Iowa. Michigan. Got. Got. Got."

"New Mexico!"

"No way!"

"Yeah. Look over there. It's got a big red sun on it.
Land of Enchantment."

"Dad! Slow down!"

Now *I'm* the Dad, and it's hard to get my kids excited
about the license plate game. Surprisingly, it's not just
because of the multitude of handheld electronic entertainment
available to them. A major blow to the game itself occurred
when states began allowing advertising. I mean, ways for
charitable organizations to raise money. Now there are far
more than fifty plate designs. Sure, it's for charity and all, but

a license plate for a cause is really just an expensive, long-term bumper sticker.

CyberDriveIllinois.com, the Secretary of State's website, shows the variety of specialty plates available to us in The Land of Lincoln. There is, of course, an additional fee, most of which goes to the organization you support when you *State Your Cause*. It'll cost $40 to show you care about *The Environment* or *Education*, or you enjoy *Cruising Route 66*. That same $40 will let you *Support Our Troops* or *Support Youth Golf*. The fees aren't standard; medical ones are a bargain. For $25, you have your choice of *Mammogram*, *Ovarian Cancer*, or *Organ Donor*. I'm not sure I want to be driving on the same road as a person that eager to support organ donation. With so many causes cast in tin, the police can't tell if the bad guy is from out of state or just *Saluting Agriculture*.

Another diversion on summer road trips that has changed slightly over the years is the interaction with the hard-working men and women of the trucking industry. When my Dad would pass a semi-trailer, he'd have to push every cylinder of the station wagon's engine. We'd lumber out into the passing lane, loaded with kids and vacation gear, hauling a popup camper with bikes piled on top. As our car crawled past the big rig, we kids would line up at the windows and try to catch the trucker's eye, by madly pumping our arms up and down, mimicking blowing his horn. If he replied with those wonderfully deafening horn blasts, we'd whoop in excitement. He'd soon blink his lights so Dad could safely move back into the right lane, and we'd wave good-bye while slowly pulling away. These days, the last thing I want my kid to do is pump his fist at a long-haul trucker as we're both rattling down the Eisenhower.

Today, kids have a variety of factory-installed video and handheld entertainment to avoid boredom on road trips. The only handheld entertainment I had as a kid were books, comics, and Mad magazines.

There's a lot of handwringing now about violence in video games, and I can see why. Judging from the sounds coming from the backseat, my son must be getting 23 kills to the mile. Although it was far less technical, the violence in my adolescent road games was far more authentic. Two words: Slug Bug. See the object, slug your opponent. Now that's an eye-hand coordination game.

Slug Bug is one game that happily has endured generations of road trips. As long as there are brothers and sisters, there will be Slug Bug. It still has to be a classic Volkswagen beetle in order to slug, no points for Jettas, but the game continues:

"Slug Bug! Red!"

"Ow! Where?"

"On the right. Turning out of that parking lot with the sign that says 'Classic Volkswagen Car Meet Today'. Hey, look at all those…"

"Oh no! Dad, speed up!"

My Heart is
Two Shades of Blue

by Larry King

Football season brings two Sundays that tear my heart apart: when the Chicago Bears play the Detroit Lions.

Growing up in Michigan, my young, impressionable, sports heart belonged to the Lions. Since moving to Chicago 30 years ago, I avidly follow the Bears and now call myself a Bears fan...along with that Lions thing. A sane person would ask, "Why bother rooting for either?"

As a kid, I cheered loudly and proudly for the team in that beautiful Honolulu Blue uniform of the Lions; thrilled by the likes of Alex Karras, Billy Sims, and George Plimpton. Plus, the lunging lion emblem on their helmets was by far the coolest in the league. But they never, ever, were a winner during my entire boyhood. Or since then, for that matter. After high school, I headed out of state to St. Joseph's College. Located deep in Indiana farmland, it had been the Bear's training camp during the 60s and early 70s. In those fertile fields, a seed was planted and I started to grow into a Bears fan.

One of St. Joe's claims to fame is that the classic, sports tearjerker movie *"Brian's Song"*, was partially filmed on campus where some of the story actually occurred. The school showed the movie every year, and I could even see my dorm room window in the background of a few scenes. And come on, it's *"Brian's Song"*! Who's not going to have a soft spot for the Bears after that? George Halas's spirit reached out to me.

Four football seasons later I got a job in Chicago, attended my first Bears game, and enjoyed it immensely. The Bears were a sports story year-round, and in those pre-internet days I received few Lions updates living 300 miles from Motown. Five seasons later, it was the '85 Super Bowl Shuffle, and the Bear was attacking the Lion. Today, after 25 more seasons following the Bears through the courtesy of their fully-supportive local media contingent, I've seen more wasted high draft picks than you can shake a general manager at, and my heart starts pumping faster when I hear "Bear down, Chicago Bears." Unfortunately, "Lie down, Detroit Lions" is also applicable, given that team's continued lack of success.

Even though I still unabashedly root for the Lions (when it's not against the Bears), I sometimes feel like a traitor. Especially every Thanksgiving back home in Michigan. Family-wise, it's the best of times as our whole clan gathers at Mom and Dad's house. Football-wise, it's usually the worst of times as the Lions do their best not to embarrass themselves on national TV, ruining turkey dinner for everyone in the state. Mom, Dad, and the five boys they raised as Lions fans all anxiously hover around the set, bemoaning that the team has only won a single playoff game in our lifetimes, and that was 18 years ago. Meanwhile, our wives are talking about something more important, which is just about anything.

I've tried to be logical when my two teams meet: root for whichever one has a better chance to make the playoffs. Some years that's like choosing between two kinds of spoiled deli meat. Other years, if one team is having an exceptionally good season and the other a lousy one, invariably an upset happens, pulling them both toward mediocrity. At least I don't have to worry about the Bears and Lions playing each other more than twice a year. That would require playoff appearances by both teams in the same season, and Las Vegas has yet to calculate odds that high.

Enduring my "civil war games" is an excruciating tangle of confusing emotions. The highlights are also the lowlights. The celebration dance is also the sigh of disappointment. My mind wanders, as I ponder the outcome of a battle between packs of real lions and bears. I'll flip channels, hoping not to see a late season baseball game between the White Sox and Tigers. In the end, I'll feel like both a winner and a loser.

After three decades in Chicago, there's a 50-yard line down the middle of my heart. I may bleed Bears Blue, but there's still a lot of Honolulu Blue in there too. With over 60 of these heart-wrenching squabbles under my belt, one thing is certain: I really hate the Packers and Vikings.

Author's Note

This story was originally written in 2010. As we go to press in Fall 2011, the Lions may have finally gotten their roar back. Crossing my fingers...on one hand.

Turf War

by Larry King

There he sits: my enemy. Perched atop the bird feeder like a general surveying the next field of conquest, his beady eyes dart in all directions. At my garden, my flower pots, my garbage cans. My territory, damn it. While not normally a nature hater, I find it difficult to live in peace with that rodent and his furry-tailed followers. What's really annoying, is he doesn't seem to realize a battle of wits is underway. Why should he care? His army of squirrels is winning.

I've seen him around for years. His tail is about half grey now, and he's slower running along the top of the fence. A big chunk of his left ear is gone, in what appears to be a bite pattern. I know he's the one in charge of all these stupid squirrels. I call him General Damit. As in, "Damn it. The squirrels dug up the flower pots." And, "Damn it. The squirrels laid waste to the watermelons." And, "Damn it. The squirrels used the barbeque and didn't even scrape the grill clean when they finished."

We have a basic suburban yard. Big enough to put up a volleyball net, not quite big enough to dive for the ball. It's been the scene of many battles between man and mini-beast. It all started with the bird feeder I put up soon after moving in. I eagerly filled it, and was surprised later in the day to see it empty. "Wow! There are some hungry birds in this neighborhood," I naively thought. Then I saw a pile of seeds below the feeder. Curious, I refilled it, got a chair, a book, a cold frosty beverage, and sat back to watch. That's when I first saw him.

He came out of nowhere and was up the pole in a blur, sitting on the feeder's ledge, helping himself. "HEY!" I yelled at him, half-lunging out of my chair. He was off like a shot across the yard and up a tree. I settled back, victorious. After this cycle happened sixteen or seventeen times, I just let him eat, and finished my beer. Little did I know that this would be the first of many times the General would lead me to drink.

I've gone through birdfeeders made of wood, plastic, steel, and titanium. None of these materials can stand up to the bayonet-sharp teeth of Damit's troops. They sit on the feeder, as if at a buffet table, picking out their favorite: the sunflower seed. As they claw through the seeds searching for this choice delicacy, the rest are scattered into a seed splatter zone, where birds eventually discover the leftovers.

This may actually make it easier for the birds, who don't care about the squirrels. They just peck their way along the ground eating whatever they find, while more seeds shower down on them. Bird and squirrel interact as if in a nature's United Nations' peacekeeping zone. In harmony, yet eyeing each other suspiciously, both ready to take flight at a moment's notice.

Still wanting to get the birds their rations with no squirrel interference, I hung a feeder in a tree. It wasn't long before The General had a squadron in formation on the branches dive-bombing the feeder.

For pole feeders, I've even considered one of those baffles which are specifically designed to keep the marauders out. It's basically an upside-down wok below the food. With my luck, they'd flip the baffle over and turn it into a 360-degree view restaurant. From there, they could look at their favorite eating establishment: my garden.

When it comes to gardening, I've found peace, tranquility, enjoyment, and success. That is, as long as I stick to crops that are not squirrel-preferred cuisine. This includes tomatoes, peas, the occasional celery, and flowers. Well, most flowers. In retrospect, knowing my enemy's love of sunflower seeds, planting giant sunflowers was not the smartest move.

The plants grew huge, some over six feet tall with stalks as big my wrist. The flowers bloomed into lovely hues of yellow, orange and red as the sun-ripened seeds burst from the flower's center. The General's advance intelligence agents must have sent word back to Headquarters, because it wasn't long before a battalion arrived. The carnage was on. Like four-legged lumberjacks, they scurried most of the way up the stalk, before their weight bent and cracked the plant in half, sending flower, stalk, seeds, and squirrels a'flying. In a flurry of teeth, claws, and squawks, they shredded the flowerheads and retreated to their encampment, jowls bulging with fresh seeds.

The sunflower strike was a quick yet devastating blow. Our Great Strawberry War lasted years and its psychological toll resounds to this day. Strawberries require a year of growth without harvest; it's just vines and leaves the first season. But I'm a patient man. The following spring when the fruit turned pink, I imagined my red, ripe, fresh strawberries soon topping an ice cream sundae. However, in a daring pre-emptive attack, the General's strike force invaded. Chittering to each other, they eviscerated the entire patch, leaving nothing but blood-red splotches of strawberry jam. He had won the battle.

I would not be deterred. A plan was hatched. Using one of humanity's greatest inventions, chicken wire, I installed an elaborate defense system for the next berry season. The following spring, I watched in delight as the squirrels ran across the raised chicken wire, instead of through the plants. When most of the berries were red and ready to be picked, I was ready too. The juicy morsels of victory awaited me under the slightly elevated chicken wire. I probably should have elevated it slightly higher. As if in a boot camp training exercise, I belly-crawled in the wet dirt under the wire, trying to avoid both the un-ripened berries and the sharp prongs, with little success. The only real harvest was scratches up and down my back, neck, arms, and legs. I left a trail of smashed berries in my wake, and sadly only got enough for half a sundae. I'm sure General Damit was overseeing it all from his secure hideout, and grinning. My strawberry fields were not forever.

The time was ripe to move on to something bigger. Pumpkins. The strawberries were torn out, and a promising pumpkin patch took its place. Toying with my emotions, the General and his minions ignored the plants for months, letting them grow as big as my false sense of security. Just as the pumpkins started turning orange, the squirrel assault was on. With near surgical precision, they carved their way in and made off with the seeds, leaving the gunk and decomposing shells. No jack-o-lanterns that year.

The next year, a friend told me that a sure way to avoid squirrel-on-pumpkin violence is to cover the pumpkins with vaseline, as the taste and texture are excellent deterrents. I was desperate enough to try, but didn't consider how strange it would look to my neighbors, when they spied me in the backyard greasing my gourds. But damned if it didn't work; the squirrels showed no interest! There was an eventual downside, however. Chemicals in the vaseline kept the pumpkins from turning orange. They were still bright green, deep into October. Martian-o-lanterns?

The pumpkins had to be de-vaselined, not an easy task. Armed with a roll of paper towels and being careful not to pull the pumpkin off the vine or step on others, I tried to wipe the goop off. Vaseline is made to be slippery, and my balance is shaky to begin with. In the sweltering Indian

Summer sun, sweat rolled into my eyes as the pumpkin I was holding grew heavier. My arms wearied, and through blurred vision I watched the pumpkin squirt out of my hands, bursting wide open upon impact. In all, I dropped two of them, stepped on one, and kicked another in frustration. At least the squirrels waited a couple of days before they destroyed the pumpkins I had managed to wipe down. Just long enough for the pumpkins to turn orange.

Perhaps trying to defeat the General and his horde isn't that great an idea. Know thy enemy? I'm afraid I might be turning into him, with all the squirrelly things I've done over the years. As I look across the yard into his beady eyes, I think maybe I'll just buy a bag of sunflower seeds, give him his own pile, and ask for a truce.

Nightly Ritual

by Larry King

She liked to do it
He didn't
Disliked it in fact
She thought it was important
Said she needed it

She was flexible by nature
It was awkward to him
She wanted to do it every night
He could go weeks without

It was becoming an issue
They needed to work it out
She pleaded and begged
He agreed to try his hardest

She was supportive and patiently guided him
He practiced on his own and confidence grew
Their hard work paid off and she was ecstatic
Now they floss together every night

Our Beloved
But Frigid Mother

by Larry King

There are a number of ways to deal with the aggravations Mother Nature throws our way in the dead of winter. Moving south is not a practical option. Here in Chicago, we sit between hundreds of miles of wind-swept Northern prairie and a huge puddle of water. It's Ma Nature's little chemistry set and she has years of experience concocting her own special brews for us. While we can never outsmart her, there are ways we can adapt to, learn from, and even embrace her chillier side.

For example, turn her howling winds into a fashion opportunity by accessorizing your already well-layered look with a scarf. Only get a real scarf. One that's heavy enough to register on a bathroom scale. Don't be taken by those hotel-bedsheet-thin neck adornments, available in colors you'll find only in a 64-crayon set. A good 50 mph arctic blast will grab that flimsy fabric and tear it away with neck-snapping force. Stay safe and save that garment for the relatively mild breezes of spring. In winter, you need a wrap that actually keeps you warm, even if it gives you the mobility of a neck brace.

Next, moving on and up, it's important to keep your ears

covered. Earlobes may be the hardest part of the body to keep warm. Those vulnerable little pinches of skin get cold and stay that way unless properly protected. Earmuffs, the headgear equivalent of galoshes, really need to be brought into the 21st century. Here's an idea: make them musical! Put earbuds in the earmuffs and enjoy your songlist in the depths of winter, all the while keeping your ears toasty warm. Call it the iMuff.

You don't need a health club when there's so much natural exercise to be had by simply stepping outside; especially, if you step outside in 12-pound boots. Ankle weights have nothing on a good pair of heavy footwear that will have your legs "feeling the burn" just by going down the driveway to pick up the mail. Add a little ambition and adventure by taking a slight detour for a more intense workout. Slog a path through the deep snow, just shuffling around the yard. Walk around the neighborhood; find a park. Take breaks to appreciate the artwork Ma Nature displays: the swirl of a snowdrift, berries stubbornly clinging to their branches while the birds eye them hungrily, the stabbing reflection off an icicle - its melting drips full of sunlight as they fall like daytime shooting stars. Eventually, head back to the mailbox, with both your cardio workout and some mental snapshots under your belt.

Another great exercise technique can be found in an unlikely place. Although winter weather conditions add tricky variables to our already stressed and idiot-overloaded traffic system, you can use that tension to your advantage. You've already got the steering wheel in a death grip. Relax. Tighten. Relax. Repeat. Do three sets of 10 each commute to develop forearms that are as toned as you wish your abs were.

Perhaps Mother Nature's most subtle, yet toughest challenge is the one that really gets on our nerves: cabin fever. Cooped-up families endure exposure to endless hours of incandescent and fluorescent fake sunlight, too much TV, and online overload. We're itching to escape. Outside, it's still a seemingly stark, dark, dead landscape. But wait...the days *are* getting longer. The temperatures *are* inching upward.

A friend has a great prescription for cabin fever: she plants flower and vegetable seeds indoors. Sprouts are soon stretching for the sun, showing the way toward the next season. Maybe that's the best lesson we can learn from Mother Nature during winter: to persevere and look forward with hope and faith, knowing brighter and warmer days are coming. We endure the difficulties she gives us and become stronger for it. Of course, come spring she may send us floods, lightning, tornadoes, blistering heat, and late snowstorms. She's dealing the cards; we're just at the table, enjoying the game as best we can.

I Have, I Am, I Wish

by Larry King

I have a friend who volunteers at a retirement community helping our more experienced citizens with computer technology. God bless her for giving her time and talents, and God bless our wise elders who have the desire to keep learning and staying in touch with the world. My friend was setting them up with Google's email product, G-mail, and asked Delores if she was ready for her G-mail account. Delores replied, "G-mail? I remember E-mail, but I must have completely missed F-mail."

I am a bad typist. Sometimes spellcheck won't save me either. At work, I was writing a document about a client's prescription drug coverage benefit, and referenced a list. Unfortunately, the keystroke "i" is next to the "u" and I unwittingly directed people to the company's "Drug Lust." Instant messaging is even worse, as I try typing faster, only compounding my handicap. I once asked a female co-worker if she was busy, but my finger hit two keys instead of one. I imagine the chill that went up her spine when my name popped onscreen, asking if she was busty today.

I wish there was a zoo for tornadoes. Those things are so impressive and so powerful yet so very deadly. But come on, they are cool. Granted, the zoo would have to be pretty big, and we'd need to have total control of the weather. Overcoming those obstacles, we could put aside a few hundred thousand acres of say, Oklahoma, and the good people of the region could set up a park full of twisters in all shapes and sizes. Hourly shows. Tell me that wouldn't be a great tourist attraction.

Wings

A Fable

By Larry King

"How did flying lessons go today, Adam?" the caterpillar asked the young sparrow.

"Good. I've got gliding completely under control, but still can't get any lift on my own," replied the bird. It hopped off the nest's ridge and down the branch toward the caterpillar, under his mother's watchful eye. "Dad says it's all in my head, but I don't think so. Clearly, he doesn't understand how embarrassing it is for a five-week old to be carried aloft by Daddy. No, I just need more wing strength."

"Oh, come on. Nobody can tell if you're three or five weeks old. You're being a little oversensitive."

"You might not be able to tell, Neil. But no offense, you're still grounded. It's a whole different ball game up there."

"No offense taken," the caterpillar said. "I'm looking forward to riding those air currents myself."

"You're going to love it. And *you* don't even have to take flying lessons! How does that work?"

"I don't know. I just know that after I make my mid-cycle shelter and fall asleep, I'll wake up ready to fly. Besides, I don't have enough time in this life cycle to ask many questions. I just enjoy it." The caterpillar began inching its way down the branch. "Speaking of which, I'm going to enjoy a nice, succulent, mulberry leaf right now. I'll see you later."

"Okay, Neil. I think I'll work on my wing strength. I need to catch up."

"Don't worry, Adam. You'll fly when it's right."

Evening had fallen by the time the caterpillar had dined, and returned to the nook in the fork of the branch where he made his home. The mulberry bush also held the sparrow nest, and the two friends were together most nights.

"Neil, you aren't going to believe who my Dad talked to over in the hedge today while he was checking out my older sister's new nest."

"Who?"

"Rufus T! And he might actually visit our bush tonight!"

"That's surprising," the caterpillar sat back, then stretched his body up in disbelief, "Why would this season's head firefly be interested in *our* bush?"

"Not our bush so much as the mulch underneath it. Dad says the fireflies have been laying eggs under the hedge for over ten seasons, and Rufus is scouting new territory. I guess once they wake up and get their wings, things happen fast."

"Oh, yes. In their cycle they only have flight for about 20 suns, after spending two seasons underground. They make the most of their time with wings. Most important, they have to get the next generation underway."

"Sleep for a couple seasons, eat, fly, mate, and glow," the young bird said enviously. "Now that's a great cycle."

"Don't be jealous of another's cycle, Adam," the caterpillar cautioned. "That's a bad road to head down. We can't all be housecats, you know."

The caterpillar began moving up the branch toward the nest when Adam's father swooped in.

"Hi, son," he said. "Rufus is on his way here. Remember

your manners when you meet him. Neil, please feel free to stay."

Approaching the bush was an on-again off-again greenish light as the firefly began his inspection of the area. After circling the bush twice, he landed on the ground and continued his review. Satisfied, he glowed brightly, then flew to the nest.

"Good evening, Mr. Sparrow," he said. "This section has a lot of potential. I hope you won't mind new neighbors."

"Not at all," replied the father bird. "We look forward to sharing the space and enjoying the light you bring. By the way, this is my son, Adam, and our neighbor, Neil."

"Pleased to meet you!" the friends said in unison.

"It's good to meet you both."

"Mr. Firefly, may I ask you something?" the young sparrow meekly chirped. "Is it true that fireflies are one of the highest forms of terrestrial life?"

"I've heard that, but don't think about it," answered Rufus. "The less we question, the more accepting, happier, and in tune with other living creatures we are. There's no need to ask a lot of questions, Adam. What are you, human?"

They all had a long and hearty laugh at that, then Rufus floated into the darkening stillness to gather his glow worms.

Holiday Cheer

by Larry King

It was hard to explain to the police why my wife Debbie and I were on our neighbor's roof with a six-foot plastic Santa and a toilet. They could probably figure out what the string of yellow lights was for. Luckily, Sid and Grace pulled into their driveway soon after the squad car did, so no charges were pressed. The officers did feel however, it was their duty to inquire about our actions. This meant not only were Deb and I busted, but the explanation had to include Sid and Grace Kimball, our neighbors and best friends. Best friends currently engaged in a series of teenage-level pranks, played by middle–aged adults. During December, our yards and houses, directly across the street from each other, had become highly visible props in a game of one-upmanship. But it was a year ago when the seed for this hissing match was planted...

Christmas Eve, last year
The Kimballs decided, after they admitted, a few too many eggnogs, to replace the Baby Jesus in our nativity scene with a plastic penguin from their winter-themed display. We didn't notice it until my in-laws, dyed-in-the-wool Catholics, pulled into our driveway for the big Christmas dinner and saw Baby Penguin in all his glory. We came up with the lame excuse that it was probably just

some neighborhood kids, but a knowing glance between my wife and me confirmed we both had different suspects in mind. Closer inspection found Baby Jesus stashed in an empty 12-pack hidden behind the manger. We laid him back in his crib and took the penguin inside.

New Year's Eve, last year

We brought the penguin to the neighborhood party where we presented it to Sid and Grace, and told how the in-laws saw it first. Everyone had a good laugh, but we warned our close pals that they better be on the lookout next Christmas. Revenge is a dish best served eleven months later.

Saturday, November 27, this year

The day was cool, dry, and perfect for putting up holiday decorations, so both houses were lit up by evening. Our tastes differ, to put it bluntly. Deb and I prefer the traditional: strings of big bulb lights around the trim of the house and garage, twinkle lights in the bushes, a wreath, and a simple manger scene. Sid's operative words are plastic, bright, and quantity. The street lights dim when his lights go on. But as friends do, you just give each other a little grief about taste and class, or lack thereof, then move on.

With all the decorating done, the four of us were in their garage having hot chocolate and hot toddies, when the previous year's Baby Jesus switcheroo came up. I reminded them of what I said on New Year's Eve about revenge, and that I'd come up with a number of interesting options. Sid laughed, but gave me a look that said "Are you serious?" I just smiled and nodded.

Sunday, November 28

I didn't have a thing. Not that there weren't enough props in their yard. Elves, reindeer, snowmen, candy canes, and Santa on a Harley were among the displays. Sid knew his layout and checked it nightly, so a simple switch would be easily detected. I needed something creative. Then I saw their TV antenna.

For a period of time between black and white television with rabbit ears, and broadband ultra-speed digitally-enhanced high definition satellite-delivered TV, steel antennas sprouted on rooftops across America like acne on a teenager. We live in a neighborhood built during that era, and most antennas haven't been taken down. The Kimball's, for example. Eventually, the antenna becomes part of the background, almost unseen. It's a perfect place to put something that might go unnoticed for a while.

Saturday, December 4

Our chance came when they went on a road trip to see Grace's parents. It didn't take much work to get the sign in place. A quick ladder to their roof, a short climb up the antenna, some fishing line, duct tape, and it was up. Not that I did it alone. Deb helped of course, as did a few neighbors, a nice little group project. Soon, most of the street was in the know, and we all eagerly awaited the Kimball's return. The sign said: "Santa, don't stop here. They've been naughty!"

Sunday, December 5

As soon as they returned, Sid was out front inspecting his display, marching up and down, finding all in order. He looked our way and said, "Hi," with a satisfied and slightly smug grin on his face.

Monday, December 13

They didn't notice for over a week. In fact, I had to sneak over after midnight and redirect one of his spotlights, pointing it up at the sign. I also unplugged their inflatable giant snow globe, knowing when their timer went on the next night they'd be down one display, sparking an inspection.

Tuesday, December 14

Sid's message on our answering machine sounded calm, but I could tell there was an edge to it. He congratulated us in a tone implying that this wasn't over. Less subtle was Grace in the background yelling, "Is that all you got? It's game on now, baby! That manger of yours is going down! Look out, Mary and Joe!"

Friday, December 17

With roles reversed, we found ourselves spending more time in the front room by the big window, watching for mischief. Nothing happened for a couple of days and it almost escaped my mind. But something looked wrong as I pulled into the driveway after work; the lights weren't quite as bright. The reason being, that every other big light bulb was out. Literally. They had been unscrewed and put into a stocking which was hung with care from a giant candy cane, stuck in the middle of the nativity scene. Clever.

Saturday, December 18, 3:00 A.M.

Deb and I intermingled their displays. Some of the elves were riding reindeer, while the rest were pitted in battle against the plastic snowmen, candy canes being the weapon of choice. The remaining reindeer appeared to be having an orgy.

Saturday, December 18, 8:37 A.M.

The message on our answering machine said simply, "Fine. Well done. But gosh, where's your precious little toilet?"

Some background on our "precious little toilet." Last spring, we replaced a toilet and instead of throwing it out, I was inspired to make a two tiered "flowerpot" for the side of the house. A little potting soil in the tank, a little more in the bowl, and pink wave petunias planted in both. I'm not sure if it was the "natural fertilizer" left over in the toilet, but the wave petunias lived up to their name, cascading down in huge bouquets, providing a unique floral and porcelain display.

One Saturday in October, I was doing both Halloween decorating and garden cleanup. The petunias were long dead, so maybe it was time to send the toilet on its delayed trip to the garbage. Not so fast. I was able to prop up a three-foot plastic skeleton so it looked like he was standing in front of the toilet relieving himself. The toilet had new life. The neighbors must have agreed, because a day or two later I noticed someone had put a plastic hand in the toilet bowl, reaching out for the skeleton. Two days later a Styrofoam tombstone appeared in the tank. Finally, the night before Halloween, the skeleton was sitting on the pot.

Of course for Thanksgiving we had to put a fake turkey on the can. We considered a number of possibilities for Christmas, but thought anything would be tacky alongside our traditional decorations. So the toilet was put on the side of our garage. But now it was gone.

Tuesday, December 21

The first snow of the season came down heavy, wet, and deep. When we went to bed, the yard was a pure winter wonderland, covered in white. We woke up to find the toilet in our front yard with a real snowman sitting on it, reading the paper. We had to admit, it looked hilarious. We also knew the toilet would have to make its way across the street. It didn't take long for us to design and build bases for the toilet and a big plastic Santa we bought, so they would sit squarely on the peak of a roof.

Thursday, December 23

A golden opportunity presented itself when the Kimballs went last minute shopping. We knew we had to be careful on the slippery, snow-covered roof, especially the area around their skylights. Help was sought and it didn't take much recruiting to get a few neighbors assembled. With Deb and I on the roof, Santa, the bases, and the string of yellow lights were handed up. Then we carefully took the toilet from two of our cohorts who lifted from below. Once up on the roof, Deb and I were able to move it to the peak with a series of lift and shift moves. The pieces were ready, we just had to set up the scene.

Nobody noticed as the police car slowly pulled up. On a routine patrol, they noticed the gathering and felt compelled to stop. The officers seemed more amused than perturbed, but an explanation was required. Thankfully, that's when Sid and Grace got home, so Deb and I came down off the roof, and the whole story came out.

The cops realized no real damage or trespassing was done, so left us with strong advice to leave the pranks to the kids, before we did something over the line that would really hurt our friendship. We agreed, and in the spirit of cooperation, Sid and I headed to the roof to bring down Santa, the lights, and the toilet. Santa and the lights made it down fine. However, the toilet was still perched precariously on the peak as we went to lift it. Unfortunately, I lifted it a half second before Sid was ready. He lost grip of the toilet tank, causing me to lose my hold on the bowl. We all watched in horror as it tumbled down the roof, accumulating snow like a giant deformed snowball headed straight toward, and then through a skylight, crashing into their living room.

A true test of friendship is how it holds up under pressure. There was some intense pressure at that point, which was relieved by a single sound: Grace laughing. The rest of us joined in; what else could we do? We called the 24-hour window repairman, split the bill, and declared a truce. Well, maybe more of a temporary cease-fire.

Seeds of Happiness

by Larry King

A pumpkin seed is an amazing thing, and not just because it's one of the few items I can cook. Fact is, I do toast up a pretty tasty batch of seeds the week after Halloween. My family and friends got hooked on the once-a-year homemade treat, so now every October I buy pumpkins by the tonnage. I enjoy the tradition, but also know that this unassuming seed has the potential to be so much more than just a crunchy snack.

If planted instead of eaten, one warm spring day the seed sends up a sprout. It cracks open the surface, unfolding a thumb-sized leaf into the air. That single green "thumbs-up" grows into yards and yards of vine, sheaves of leaves, and a bounty of big orange gourds. Each gourd holds scores of seeds: the next pumpkin generation. Pumpkins make rabbits look like reproduction slackers.

Make no mistake, this seed is truly a powerhouse of growth, and the backyard gardener risks losing most of his "acreage" to the invasive pumpkin plant. Its green tentacles and elephant-ear sized leaves crawl across the landscape, surrounding and engulfing innocent pepper and tomato plants. Sadly, it's a crapshoot as to how many gourds actually appear. There are male and female plants, so if the bees and butterflies don't help with pollination, you're out of luck. If you're fortunate enough to have lots of fruit, it's possible they'll be gutted by a gang of vicious neighborhood squirrels. That usually happens about two weeks before Halloween. More than once those furry-tailed rats have broken my heart. Growing your own pumpkin seeds is a risky endeavor.

That's why I'm usually looking for inexpensive pumpkins in late October. I avoid any store or stand that sells pumpkin by the pound, sticking with places that price by size: small, medium, large, and I-just-hurt-something-picking-it-up. The key to purchasing pumpkins is to think ahead. In fact, think specifically of a head you want to create when you're carving. A squat, chubby face? Frankenstein-shaped noggin? It's important to think outside the patch. A pumpkin with a flat side is an orange opportunity. Lay it on its side and the stem becomes a perfect nose. You could have a hook nose, an uppity nose, a stub nose. Who knows what kind of nose you will find! Plus, this approach lets you cut the main access hole in the pumpkin's bottom, resulting in easier cleaning.

Ah, the cleaning. Goopy, gooey, gross, and snotty. Sort of what I feel like with a nasty cold. But that's the gunk you have to deal with to get at those precious seeds. Sometimes they come out in clumps, grape-like in their bunching. Mostly, they seem intent on escape, squirting out of my fingers or clinging to the stringy pulp.

After the seeds are separated from the rest of the guts, it's time to carve Mr. Jack O'Lantern. A round, slick, heavy object. Slimy, slippery hands. And various razor-sharp, steel-bladed knives. Perhaps not the most intelligent combination. I imagine emergency rooms see a sharp rise in self-inflicted knife-on-hand wounds in late October. The telltale sign of the injury's source is orange-stained skin around the cut. Accidents aside, faces are sculpted into the pumpkins, candles are lit, and the fun of Halloween glows from the inside of what had just been a seed repository.

The seeds are cleaned, strained, and soaked in salt water. The number of hours, okay, days they soak depends on how busy the rest of life is. Eventually the seeds get to the roasting tray, a final layer of salt is sprinkled on, the oven is cranked to 375, and it's toasting time. Some pop, actually. Nothing like Orville Redenbacher, but a few flop around as they heat up. For those that don't, I use a spatula to flip them halfway through. Each tray differs in how evenly-cooked and crunchy the seeds are, depending on how long they're in the oven. That depends on what's on TV.

I then go into drug dealer mode: dividing the seeds into equal portions, putting them in plastic baggies, and making the rounds to my friends, dropping off their stash. At each stop, I see the same excited look on their face as when my family gobbles the seeds fresh from the oven: pure, instantaneous happiness.

For me, that's the most amazing thing about a pumpkin seed. It allows me to give a little gift of joy.

Larry King

ALISA KOBER

Alisa's Acknowledgements:

My mother is a teacher. I am a game developer. I figure we balance each other out. She gives the kids homework and I distract them from doing it. Job security at its finest.

I've always had a creative, yet slightly subversive side and knew before making my way through the public school system in Arlington Heights and my studies at The School of the Art Institute of Chicago that I would be a professional artist...with a twist. Now, I animate characters running, jumping, and clobbering each other in the head for a living. If you are interested in seeing my work, check out www.alisakober.com.

As an animator, I enjoy bringing characters to life. As a writer, I have the same goal. My contributions to this collection include character studies rich in emotion, dialog, and humor. I hope you will enjoy them.

I'd like to thank my parents, Doris Kober and the late Kenneth Kober, for always encouraging me to pursue my creative tendencies. Also, the "Panera" gang and the "Folio" group for being the most supportive writing groups ever. And thanks to my soul mate Brian, who understands the desire to create more than anyone. You are my inspiration.

ALISA KOBER

Just Visiting

by Alisa Kober

I'd never been to a loony bin before. Not that it hadn't been suggested. In jest, of course. I think. My college roommate, Gina, on the other hand, landed a second floor suite at "Crazies 'R' Us" after her malnourished brain finally triggered the self-destruct button.

I pulled into the visitor lot of the behavioral health hospital, parked, and turned off the motor. Sleet scratched diagonally through the spotlights pelting the open armed Jesus statue near the entrance.

The girls on my floor had said I was nuts for braving the icy roads tonight. But I'd certainly go crazy if I didn't see Gina and make sure she was okay. Not hospital lock-down crazy, but still. When your R.A. informs you that your roommate was taken away in an ambulance, what are you supposed to do? Start rearranging the furniture, grab more closet space and drink all the Diet Coke in the mini-fridge? Were the other girls on my floor vultures? Jesus Christ.

I looked at the illuminated statue, towering above me. "Sorry," I muttered aloud. Great. Now I'm talking to inanimate objects. My grip tightened on the steering wheel as I stared at the oversized so-called savior. Gina believes in You though. Fat lot-a good it did her. And if her attempt had succeeded...some followers think her soul would be condemned to hell. Talk about insanity.

I don't even know who I'm mad at. God? Gina? Maybe myself?

Ice already coated the windshield so I turned the key, flipped the wiper blades on and looked up at the hospital. The building was three stories of institutional concrete with wire reinforced windows. An older building. The wire glass a bad choice. My Building Structural Systems professor would have a fit. Reinforced wire glass would certainly make escape difficult, but it shatters and could injure patients. It was meant to deter break-ins. It certainly wouldn't protect those trying to break out.

Now I'm just stalling, and it's already eight-o-clock.

I just don't know how I could have missed the warnings. Were there any? It's not like Gina gave me her music collection or gifted me her laptop. Sure, she was struggling— her daily routine was run, not eat, classes, not eat, study, and not eat. But we still laughed along with our favorite "Must See TV" and gossiped about meaningless crap. I figured she'd get weak from lack of calories, maybe pass out and finally get help.

No. I should have known. Should have done something. Was I waiting for an "Out of milk, P.S. Going to kill myself today" note tacked up to the bulletin board?

I forced myself out of the car and headed for the entrance. Sleet coated the walkway with a slippery film so I granny-walked my way between the melty spots created by salt clumps. Wouldn't want to break a leg here. It's not that kind of hospital.

I made it to the building, bones intact. At the reception area, an aquarium wall filled with beautiful tropical fish camouflaged a head-top, which peeked out from behind the large barrier reef of a desk.

The head-top spoke. "Can I help you?"

"Hi. I'm here to visit a patient. Gina Pearson."

The receptionist typed in the name. "And you are?"

"Sarah Zimmerman."

She made a note and then handed me a clipboard holding a sign-in sheet and a pen on a string. There were only five other names on the list for the day. Not many visitors braved the weather it seemed. Sad.

I signed in and handed the clipboard back. The receptionist checked the computer screen again and then handed me a visitor sticker. "North wing. Second floor. Through the doors you'll see an elevator to your left."

As I affixed the visitor sticker to my chest, I looked around the small lobby. No gift shop to purchase "get well" trinkets. No vending machines. Just a small entryway with a few chairs, admitting office to the right, an unlit chapel to the left and a large locked double set of white doors past the reception desk. Other than the sanitarium aquarium, the place was not very inviting.

I approached the double doors and heard a buzzing and a click, which allowed me passage inside the tightly secured facility.

At least the people here should be able to help Gina. I hope. They're probably trained to see past her smile to the troubled soul behind it. She was good at faking it though. Always cheerful with the "everything's fine" mask firmly in place.

I'd gotten better at interpreting her actual condition after rooming with her for the last six months. When asked how she was, a response of "fine" was typical. It meant she was not in fact fine, but was coping in a state of oblivious denial. Even an answer of "okay" was nothing to be concerned with unless the emphasis was on the "o". "OOH-kay" meant she was struggling. But at least she knew it and would be open to talking about it. You only really had to worry if she was "good," or worse yet, "great." She must have been feeling "fabulous" this afternoon.

Stepping off the elevator on the second floor, I was confronted by a long hallway with the kind of carpeting I would expect to see in a movie theater. Wear resistant. Colorful with a dizzying pattern to hide incidental spills and stains. But in this bright utilitarian light, it seemed garish, distracting, and made the floor of the hallway alive with movement.

Another security door blocked my passage so I rang the "Ring for Admittance" bell. A bouncer-sized orderly opened the door.

"May I see your bag, Miss?" he asked.

I handed over my purse and he rummaged through it, checking every compartment. Checkbook, credit card, student ID, car keys. And Yep! Those are tampons.

"Sure is nasty weather out there tonight," he said.

I just nodded. I didn't feel like discussing the weather.

After my purse and pockets had been meticulously checked for any floor-banned items or "sharps," the orderly let me continue through a second set of locked doors to the family room.

So, this was it. This was where they hide people when society deems them abnormal. A risk to themselves or others. Lunatics.

The family room was sparsely planted with patients staring at the wall-mounted television. Some nature show. A patient was suddenly standing next to me.

"I love animals," a short, dark-complexioned woman said, elongating her words. She stood really close, an assault to my personal space and olfactory senses. Her bright smile grinned unnaturally at me so I scanned the room and adjoining halls to see if I could spot Gina.

Would she be awake? Lucid? Curled up in a corner rocking back and forth?

A familiar face looked toward me from a pay phone about fifty feet down the hall. Gina smiled and held up a finger indicating she would be off the phone in a minute, looking perfectly normal. I exhaled in relief.

"Excuse me." I maneuvered past the grinning woman and edged around a stack of chairs marked "Housekeeping–please clean." Gina was still on the phone so I took my time making my way down the hall.

Jeeze. You could become lost staring into the carpet. The simulated vegetation and intricate, tangling vines repeated diagonally, bouncing back and forth from wall to wall, down the long corridor.

It made me wonder about the administrator responsible for the décor decisions. Probably a well-adjusted business person concerned with the cost effectiveness of materials used, never realizing the impact and distress the patients must experience when the floor rises up to greet them. I hope they picked a plainer pattern for the detox floors. I was getting dizzy.

As I moved toward Gina, I noticed an enclosed room with two walls of glass across from the nurse's station. A haze of smoke swirled and settled as people paced through it, back and forth, left and right, smoking cigarettes. The atmosphere contained behind the glass looked steamy and thick. People moved inside as if they were slowed by a heavy humidity. Maybe it was like a rain forest. That might explain the tropical carpeting.

One of the pacers extinguished his cigarette stub in the ashtray, instantly pulling a new one from the pack. Placing it between his lips, he walked over to the wall and placed the tip of it into an appliance of some kind. Fresh smoke was sucked from the other end.

I was confused for a moment and then realized. Ah. No lighters... Fire hazard.

I walked over to the pay phones and briefly hugged Gina as she attempted to finish her conversation. It was unusual for her to be wearing a short sleeve T-shirt. It exposed her arms, which were thin and carried only the necessary bone and muscle needed to function. Her left wrist was neatly bandaged.

I also rarely ever saw Gina without shoes. She had Nike runners strapped to her feet nearly twenty-four-seven. Even slept in them sometimes. Her closet at the dorm is crammed with shoeboxes like she robbed a Foot Locker. Many of the boxes are identical too, containing reserves of her favorite model of performance running shoe, now discontinued.

She noticed me staring at her feet – stark white socks against the crazy colored carpet.

Gina pulled the phone from her ear and covered the receiver. "Yeah. No shoes... Laces." She pantomimed grabbing a necktie and hoisting it over her head.

Ah. Nothing like gallows humor to brighten up a trip to the funny farm.

"It will be fine. He probably just had a bad day."

She must be talking to her sister.

"No. He won't move out." Pause. "Because he cares about you. Why do you always think it's your fault?"

What was with the old pay phones anyway? Cruel. Calls can come in but patients need coins to call out. Who the hell would think to bring change?

"No. You're not." Pause. "Look. I have to get off the phone, someone else needs to use it."

Would her sister be upset if she knew she had a visitor? Makes me wonder if the wrong sister wasn't locked up. Give her a break. She's in a mental hospital for Christ's sake! I certainly wouldn't be crying to my sister about a minor spat with a husband at a time like this.

"Sorry," she said, finally hanging up.

"I understand," I pretended.

"You didn't have to come all the way out here. I'm fine."

"I know." There was no point in arguing.

"Does it hurt?" I nod toward her bandaged wrist. The

image of traced veins still makes my chest tight.

"No. Just a scratch." She smiled, but it faded quickly when I didn't laugh along. "I'm sorry. I'm the shittiest roommate ever. I didn't plan to. It just sort of happened."

Gina had been found bleeding in a corner of a dark lecture hall in the Psych department. Ironic? Yes. Something that "just happened?" I doubt it.

"You could have talked to me." I reached out and took her left hand in mine.

"I know."

"You know I'd do anything to help, don't you?"

"Yeah." Gina's eyes would not meet mine. They just stared off into the middle space. Sometimes I would come home from class and she would be in the bathroom washing her hair...for an hour, until the water ran cold. Or staring at the same textbook page or at the clothes in her closet for extended periods. There was a lost look that would blink away as soon as you said her name.

"Gina? Were you worried about going home for spring break?" I asked.

"I don't know. Maybe." Her eyes connected with mine then started to glaze over again.

"Well, you picked a fine place for an alternative vacation." I kidded, trying to bring her back. "Fine tropical scenery." I dramatically presented the carpeting. "Interesting natives." I furtively glanced over at some guy mumbling to himself as he passed us. "And the best drugs insurance can buy."

Gina laughed. "Just don't sit in any of the chairs."

"Why?"

"Sherry over there tends to pee on them." Gina pointed to the overly smiley woman I had met when I entered.

"Yikes."

"I'm not actually supposed to be here, you know."

Did she actually believe that?

"No, not that," she back-peddled. "I mean I'm not

supposed to be in this wing."

"You mean the pee-your-pants, perpetual smoking, maximum security wing?"

"Yeah - the South wing is full. Over there it's all eating disorders, cutters, and substance abuse folks. I'll be moved there as soon as a bed opens up."

"How long are you in for?"

"At least a week, and then I'll continue as an out-patient in the day program." She looked a little lost in thought. "I just don't want to miss too many classes."

"There will be plenty of time for school when you're better."

A nurse came by to let us know we needed to wrap it up. It was already eight-thirty. The weather had made getting here a nightmare. I should have left earlier. The staff had warned me that visiting hours were only seven to eight-thirty on weekdays.

"I'm sorry I was on the phone so long," Gina sighed. "My sister is so insecure."

Said the girl who refused to date to avoid having to worry about her appearance and what to wear, say, and do.

"I just had to see how you were doing. I called, but no one would even confirm that you were here at first, let alone okay."

"Yeah. No information... Confidentiality."

I dug in my purse and grabbed a handful of change. The copper-colored ones went back. The rest was for her. "Call me if you need anything."

"They keep us pretty busy and only allow calls at certain times, but I'll try."

"Try. Call me soon. Thursday night comedies won't be the same without you," I said hugging her goodbye. "Please, take care of yourself."

"I just want my shoes."

"I know."

I felt so bad leaving her. I squeezed her hand then pulled

away.

The white-coated man guarding elevator access opened the door as I approached. Gina hung back and waved meekly. She didn't have a visitor sticker.

"The roads look pretty bad," the guard observed out the window as we walked to the next set of security doors. "Don't wanna get snowed in."

Good God, no. "It's pretty icy. It took me over an hour to get here from the university."

He paused at the second security door. "You could always stay." He smirked and pointed back to the family room. Sherry's face was pressed up against the locked door's window, her bright smile gleaming like a Cheshire cat. "Sherry has an empty bed in her room. I think she likes you."

I must have looked horrified because he started laughing.

"I'm just messing with ya, sweetheart," he opened the door. "You drive safe now."

I am SO out of here!

The elevator was empty and slow. I looked up and watched as the "2" grew dark and waited for the "1" to light. I imagined being trapped between floors, claustrophobic. That would figure. Of all places it would happen here. I'd wig out and have a panic attack, then be dragged upstairs, sticker revoked.

One. One. One! The dark in-between time was drawn out like a fatal doctor diagnosis or a game show host confirming... "Final answer?" My heart beat rapidly, ticking off the seconds.

"Ding!" The one lit.

Open. Open. Open!

The door seemed to pause for dramatic effect before finally releasing me from the airless box.

Jesus.

Ground floor. Show's over. Please exit to the right.

I breathed a sigh of relief and headed for the large double doors, which were my exit. The small wire re-enforced window framed the lobby. I rang the bell, hand poised on the door handle. There was no buzzing sound. A sign read, "Stand in front of camera and show badge." I complied and rang the bell again. The door remained locked.

Again. No answer.

I knocked. Silence.

The main floor looked deserted. Was there no one at the front desk? Visiting hours just ended. It's not like I stayed too long. Why were there no other visitors? Had they already left? The weather was bad tonight. Freezing rain and fog.

I'm locked in. I started to sweat.

I rang the bell again and waved my visitor sticker in front of the camera. Maybe they were double-checking. It wouldn't be hard for a patient to slap on a sticker and fake out the guards.

A staff person approached. He reached toward me. I closed my eyes.

"Excuse me," he said reaching past me with his security card to the sensor. The door clicked and opened. He was just a staff member finishing his shift. I was an idiot, but relieved when he held the door for me.

As I walked out, the receptionist exited the bathroom. She waved goodnight to the other staff member and resumed her post under the sea.

Stepping outside, I wrapped my coat tightly around myself.

I looked up at the second floor windows. It killed me to leave Gina there. But it was for the best, right?

I headed for the car. Glad to be wearing my shoes.

Refusing to Wake Up

by Alisa Kober

Jessica rolls to the vacant side of her bed. The visitor's side: the space she claims as her own, most nights.

Looking over the edge of the mattress, she sees clothes discarded carelessly on the once vacuum-patterned carpet, the contents of the pockets spilled out onto the rug among wads of used tissue. The white wicker wastebasket sits, unappreciated.

The shower is running. He will be leaving soon.

She's been dating Rick for a few months. Before that, there was Jason, the rugby player, and before Jason, there was Matt, a frat boy who had introduced her to the sexual freedom of college life and then never called. What an asshole.

Rick is different. A Junior. Much more mature. He doesn't email her pictures of his junk after three a.m. benders. A definite step up.

Jessica is so glad that she moved out of the freshman dorms. Her new roommates are totally cool. She now has her own room, shares the bathroom with three girls instead of an entire floor, plus, she can have overnight guests without hassle.

Jessica hears Rick clear his throat, cough up phlegm, and then spit. She was going to clean the bathroom today anyway. Her roommates would not be thrilled to find body hair left in the tub. She cringes, imagining the short hairs left on the soap to re-congeal into the bar. She hopes he's not using Cheryl's loofah again.

Pulling the covers back to free her legs, she swings them around to dangle, while she rubs the images from her eyes. Rick is a cuddly teddy bear, well worth the disturbance of her pristinely clean and organized space. She loves waking up next to him, his broad shoulders cradling her head against his chest.

Jessica stretches her neck left... Crack. Then right... Crack. Time to wake up.

Standing, she sighs. Her foot encounters a cold squishy something. Taking a fresh tissue from the box, she picks up the used condom under her feet, not wanting to touch this now vile thing directly.

Judging by the sounds of humming and lathering, the final rinse has not begun. She has a few more minutes before he will be politely excusing himself to an early morning class.

Retrieving a fresh T-shirt and underwear, Jessica dresses. The shirt hangs loosely from her breasts. She tames her wild hair and pops a mint Tic-Tac into her mouth.

She makes the bed, arranging the shammed pillows into a pleasingly neat configuration.

Begging to be rescued from their rumpled state, his khaki pants are left alone, despite her overwhelming urge to straighten pleats, fold, and smooth the cloth.

She's not his mother. Nor is she his wife...well, someday... maybe.

The bathroom door opens and a toweled Rick enters through the steam. He kisses her, then quickly dresses himself leaving the wet towel on the floor next to the bed.

"Gotta go babe," he says. "Saturday morning classes suck."

"Will I see you tonight?" Jessica asks.

"Don't know." Rick walks out of the bedroom and down the hall. Jessica trails after him. He fills a travel mug from the coffee pot and caps it tightly. "I have to see what the guys are up to." With that, he picks up his backpack and heads for the exit, stopping briefly to survey the contents of the fridge. He grabs an apple and stuffs it in his face. "I'll ca' ya later," he mumbles through a mouth full of produce.

After he leaves, Jessica walks to the window and watches him swagger toward campus. She smiles and waves, unable to smell the coffee.

Slice of Life with Pepperoni

by Alisa Kober

The smack talk was flying around the apartment as A.J. and Lawrence tested each other's dexterity and gaming prowess. Sweaty hands gripped controllers as button combos were traded along with insults.

"Oh yeah! Dragon Punch to the virtual nads, my friend!"

Lawrence's on-screen character recuperated, health bar indicating a dire situation. "Chun-Li has no nads, Doofus." With clenched teeth, Lawrence went on the offensive, furiously maneuvering in for the kill. Fingers flying over the buttons, he launched a super move, pummeling A.J.'s character in a blur of legs and panties. "Legs of lightning, baby!"

"Son of a bitch!" A.J. jumped to his feet sending the controller to the ground with a crash.

"It's not the controller you scrawny hack. You just suck!" Lawrence teased, reaching for his beer.

"Judge me by my size do you? I'll school you in Street Fighter Real, doughboy!" A.J.'s pants interrupted with a Foo Fighters song. He pulled his phone from his pocket and retrieved the incoming text message. It simply read... PICK UP 9:15. "Hot Damn! Gotta go to work."

"I thought you were done delivering for the night?"

"I am. This is a pick-up!"

"Huh? Oh, you mean of the medical professional kind." Lawrence set his controller down with a frown. Game night would be temporarily interrupted. "I think female hospital employees are already inoculated against tetanus, hepatitis B, and twenty-eight year old pizza delivery guys. Why must you torture yourself?"

"Love is no longer bound by social classes and cultural tradition." A.J. sauntered to the door, grabbing his keys from the hook on the wall.

"Really? Tell my mother that." Lawrence took a long drink from a can of Bud.

A.J. sniffed his pits, ran a hand through his wavy dark hair and centered his lucky red baseball cap atop his head. A knock on the door met A.J. on his way out. Their nerdy neighbor Todd was on the other side, arms loaded with electronics, wires and cables. "Who wants free satellite T.V.?" he asked, grinning sheepishly in the doorway.

"Oooh! Me!" Lawrence said getting to his feet slowly and hiking up his sweat pants.

"Todd-O-Vision coming right up!"

"You two pirates can wallow in your material treasures," A.J. dismissed. "I seek greater things."

"Tits?" Lawrence gargled, mid beer.

"Love, you fools. Love! That to which no amount of Skin-O-Max can compare." A.J. left apartment 305 and headed for the stairs, car keys twirling around his index finger. "Later, losers."

Things were looking up. Another chance to make a favorable impression on his favorite customer. Lawrence had given up on women. And Todd? He had probably never even spoken to one unless it was in Klingon. A.J. was proud that he was at least trying. Sure, he might be out of his league, but at least it was better than succumbing to stereotypes and wallowing his underemployed life away in the World of Warcraft.

A.J. pulled his clunky Volkswagen Thing into a parking spot behind Lou's Pizza. The bright red Camaro Z28 by the back door told him that Tim was on late shift delivery tonight. It wasn't until A.J. approached the door that he actually saw Tim, a short fellow, leaned up against his car perusing the latest Maxim magazine. Tim had been delivering for Lou for years.

"Hey, Timbo!"

"I thought you were off for the night?"

"Got a pick-up!" A.J. raised and lowered his eyebrows, a smirk on his face.

"Who? That nurse chick, Beth? Dream on, slacker." Tim focused back on his magazine.

As soon as he was inside, A.J. flipped through all of the order tickets hanging on the line. Where was it? Where was her order?

"Whatcha looking for?" Lou ripped the next order tag off the line before A.J. could read it.

"Come on Lou. Where's her order?"

"Patience, Romeo. I got it right here." Lou stapled the tag to the top of the pizza he just boxed and stored it above the ovens. "She should be here any minute. Gotta game plan?"

"Casual non-threatening charm, coupled with my charismatic good looks should do the trick. And forming complete sentences this time."

A.J. opened the cooler and helped himself to a Mountain Dew as the phone rang.

Lou just shook his head. "Hey! That ain't no free beverage dispenser. Make yourself useful and answer that, will ya?"

A.J. picked up the receiver and punched the button for line one. "Lou's Pizza. Will this be for pick-up or delivery?"

There was a pause on the line. "Um...yeah. What size

do you have?"

"We have small, medium, and large in thin, thick, deep, or stuffed."

"...I heard you have a tiny one." Pre-teen giggles surged from the receiver before the line went dead.

"Aw. Burn!" A.J. yelled, throwing the blank order tickets to the side. "All right you little shits! Feel the wrath of caller I.D." A.J. dialed *69. Prank vengeance would be his.

Someone pushed the front door of the pizzeria open, ringing the bell. "Uh... A.J.?" Lou whispered. "You got a customer..."

A.J. waved his hand absently in recognition, not noticing Lou's strained face, frantic pointing and wide eyes. After five rings, someone at the prankster's house finally picked up.

"Hello?" It was an older woman's voice.

"Hello." A.J. checked the caller I.D. display. "Mrs. Peterson?"

"Yes."

"May I ask you a question?"

"Okay..."

A.J. grabbed the walk-in customer's pizza from Lou and rang up the order automatically, continuing his phone call. "Mrs. Peterson, I wanted to ask if you beat your children."

"Heaven's NO!" the earpiece screeched.

"If I give you twenty bucks, will you start?" A.J. made change for the customer, cradled the phone mouthpiece down on his shoulder and passed the receipt and change across the counter. "Have a nice da..."

A tall woman in scrubs took her change and pizza with a quizzical look. "Um...you too." Then she turned and walked out of the restaurant, the bell signaling her departure.

A.J. stood slack jawed and motionless as the muffled sounds of an irate mother screamed "Who the *HELL* is this?" into his shoulder. Beth drove off into the night, the round tail lights of her Bug disappearing into the distance.

A.J. put the receiver back up to his ear. "Look, Ma'am. I'm sure your boys are angels, but could you please inform them that it's impolite to prank call a place of business and make dick jokes? We'd all appreciate it." A.J. hung up and walked back to the prep area. He lowered his head to the table with a thunk.

"I tried to warn you." Lou stated as he boxed a pizza for delivery and hit the bell signaling for Tim.

"I always come off as a total asshole!" A.J. thumped his head on the table repeatedly. "I blew it. AGAIN! She must think I am the total loser that I am."

"Aw, don't sweat it." Lou consoled. "There is always a next, next time."

A.J. sighed as he turned the key to apartment 305. Lou had been kind enough to send him home with a free no-show pizza, a small consolation to his romantic catastrophe.

When he opened the door, it looked like an electronics bomb had gone off. There were parts strewn all over the living room. Dusty boxes, wires, cables, and controllers from every gaming console known to man, lay like rubble from a war-torn Game Stop. His roommate Lawrence sat in the middle of it like a captain surveying his booty.

"Ahoy! Permission to come aboard?" A.J. inquired, gingerly stepping through the mess toward the kitchen counter.

Todd was on his knees, screwdriver in hand. "A.J.! I've installed the latest direct digital receiver with 110 watts per channel, and a 100 dB signal-to-noise ratio. Once the dish is aligned, you'll have up to 5000 channels broadcasting from 33 different countries...plus Texas."

A.J. picked his way through the piles of crap, sending a stack of Atari 2600 cartridges cascading to the floor. "Where the hell did all this come from?"

"Storage," Lawrence's voice emanated from behind the piles.

"I feel like I'm on an episode of Hoarders," A.J. said, overwhelmed.

"No. Check this out!" Lawrence climbed out from behind a shelf stacked with consoles. "It's our very own evolutionary shrine of digital entertainment, arranged in archeological order."

"Sweet Jesus...Is that a Turbo Grafix 16 system?"

"Complete with add on CD, 'Beyond Shadow Gate' and an import of 'Space Adventure Cobra'!"

Todd put a hand on A.J.'s shoulder. "A superior machine which fell along with the Beta format. Sad, really."

"Beta?" A.J. looked confused.

Lawrence sighed. "It was one of the first video tape formats, moron. But the porn industry adopted the VHS tape format, so guess who won?"

"Porn?"

"Exactly."

Coiling up a bunch of cables, Todd picked his way through the mess toward the door. "I'll be up on the roof aligning the dish if you need me." He closed the door behind him.

Lawrence studied A.J.'s bewildered face. "So. How did your pick-up go?"

A.J. cleared a space and flopped down on the couch, pulling his hat over his eyes. "Ugg. Don't remind me."

"Hold a sec. I need another beer." Lawrence lifted himself from the piles of game components and pushed his way through to the kitchen.

"I was taking a call...when she came in...and I was distracted."

"Man was not meant to multi-task." Lawrence rummaged through the fridge, extracting two beers.

"But, I...how could I have...been so oblivious?"

Lawrence handed A.J. a cold one and sat down next to him. "We are stupid. It's a fact. Get use to it. Men are one track thinkers without the cognitive ability to formulate complex integrated solutions to problems when confronted with the female of the species." Lawrence took a sip of beer, thoughtfully. "If we could, we'd have invented a dietary supplement that makes cum taste like chocolate."

A.J. nearly spit from laughter and forced himself to swallow the mouthful of beer. He looked at Lawrence, a neo Budda in his presence. "My God. You're a genius."

"Nobel peace prize here we come." They clinked beer cans in a toast.

"Look, dealing with women is simple." Lawrence grabbed one of the nearby boxes and pulled out a handful of Star Wars figures. "See." He held a Slave Girl Leia figure in one hand and Han Solo in the other. "A confident guy goes out into the world, asks out ten girls a night, and goes home with one." He dropped Han and picked out Snaggletooth. "Guys like you might ask out ten girls a year. It's a numbers game."

"Snaggletooth? Really?" A.J. protested. "I'm way taller. I'm at least a Wookiee. And besides, if I just wanted 'A girl' I could probably land one." A.J. pictured Beth, her sweet demeanor, deep brown eyes, a screamin' bod that even baggie scrubs couldn't mute.

"She's out of yer league, dude," Lawrence shook his head and smiled.

"I know, I know, but..."

"The heart wants what the heart wants."

"Exactly," A.J. sighed. "I guess I'll give it one more shot. Maybe two."

Lawrence smiled then turned his head toward the kitchen, nose in the air. "Speaking of what the heart wants, do I smell free pizza?"

Alisa Kober

Typography
makes a difference.

The body of this book is set in
Bookman Old Style™
by Ong Chong Wah
for The Monotype Corporation

Selected text is set in
Arial
by Robin Nicholas, Patricia Saunders,
Steve Matteson and others
for Monotype Typography.

...featuring

Yank

by S. John Ross
of CumberlandGames.com

Telidon Condensed Heavy Italic
by Ray Larabie
of Typodermic Fonts

and
James Paul
by James Fajardo
of Fajardo

Their art is our stage. With thanks.

"It takes a heap of sense to write good nonsense."
Mark Twain

"If you want to change the world, pick up your pen and write."
Martin Luther

To You,
Our Reader-

Did you enjoy this collection?

We write to engage our readers,
and we are hoping to hear from you.
If you would like to get in touch,
send us a note at:

WritersPage.AlmanacLocal.com/aha.html

Would you like additional copies of this volume?
Would you like them autographed or personalized?
Or would you like to be notified of upcoming volumes?
Let us know!
Please note that we never share our list with anyone.
To be removed, just ask.

In the meantime, look for more of our work
*in **The Almanac of Arlington Heights***
(that 'Little Yellow Book'),
on sites around the net
and in print.

Thank you for your interest!

CPSIA information can be obtained at www.ICGtesting.com
Printed in the USA
LVOW081118300412

279684LV00002B/34/P